Eyewitness
BIRD

Pheasant wing

Crow egg

Guillemot egg

Magpie egg

Wagtail nest

Mallard wing

Peacock tail
covert

Budgerigar feathers

Dunnock egg   Great tit egg

Eyewitness
BIRD

In association with
THE NATURAL HISTORY MUSEUM

Written by
DAVID BURNIE

Tawny owl skull

Mandarin duck display feather

Quail egg

Swallow egg

Blackbird skull

Golden pheasant cape feathers

Kittiwake egg

Macaw flight feather

Avocet skull

Swallow egg

Jay wing feather

Bird of paradise display feathers

DK
DK Publishing

Partridge egg

Curlew skull

DK

LONDON, NEW YORK, MELBOURNE,
MUNICH, and DELHI

Project editor Janice Lacock
Art editor Carole Ash
Managing art editor Jane Owen
Special photography Peter Chadwick, Kim Taylor
Editorial consultants The staff of the
Natural History Museum, London

REVISED EDITION
Managing editors Andrew Macintyre, Camilla Hallinan
Managing art editors Jane Thomas, Martin Wilson
Editors Angela Wilkes, Sue Nicholson
Art editor Catherine Goldsmith
Consultant Mark Fox
Publishing manager Sunita Gahir
Category publisher Andrea Pinnington
Production Jenny Jacoby, Angela Graef
Picture research Brenda Clynch
DTP designers Siu Chan,
Andy Hilliard, Ronaldo Julien
U.S. editor Elizabeth Hester
Senior editor Beth Sutinis
Art director Dirk Kaufman
U.S. DTP designer Milos Orlovic
U.S. production Chris Avgherinos

This Eyewitness ® Guide has been conceived by
Dorling Kindersley Limited and Editions Gallimard

This edition first published in the United States in 2008
by DK Publishing, 375 Hudson Street, New York, NY 10014

A catalog record for this book is
available from the Library of Congress.

ISBN 978-0-7566-3768-2 (HC) 978-0-7566-0657-2 (Library Binding)

Color reproduction by Colourscan, Singapore
Printed and bound by Leo Paper Products Ltd., China

Discover more at
www.dk.com

Green woodpecker wing

Curlew
feather

Pheasant
feather

Wild turkey
feather

Flamingo
feather

Parrot skull

Robin egg

Razorbill egg

Contents

Rock pebbler feather

Cockatiel feather

Budgerigar feather

From dinosaur to bird

An artist's impression of *Archaeopteryx*

In 1861, QUARRY WORKERS in southern Germany discovered one of the world's most famous fossils. Called *Archaeopteryx*, it had feathers and wings – the unmistakeable hallmark of a bird. However, unlike any modern bird, *Archaeopteryx* also had a bony tail and sharp claws on its wings. Stranger still, it also had dozens of tiny pointed teeth – the same shape as ones found in dinosaurs. Experts were astounded. Here was strong evidence that birds evolved from dinosaurs over 150 million years ago. Since then, many more discoveries have helped to back this up. They include fossils of "dino-birds" from China, which had a covering of furry feathers – probably to help them keep warm. At some point in the distant past, these small, fast-running predators gave rise to the first real birds, which had flight feathers and wings, enabling them to get off the ground. Today, there are over 9,500 species of birds, ranging from hummingbirds that could sit in a matchbox, to the ostrich, which is up to 9 ft (2.7 m) tall. Thanks to their feathers and wings, birds live all over the world and they dominate the skies.

THE MISSING LINK

Since the 1860s, 10 different fossils of *Archaeopteryx* have been found. All of them come from Solnhofen in Germany – a region famous for its fine-grained limestone. This part of Europe was once flooded by a shallow sea. When animals died, their bodies were often washed into the water and gently buried by silt. As the silt built up, it slowly hardened, turning the remains into fossils. This fossil is the "Berlin *Archaeopteryx*," which was discovered in the 1870s. Its wings and legs are beautifully preserved and so are the outlines of its feathers. It is one of the few *Archaeopteryx* fossils with the head still intact.

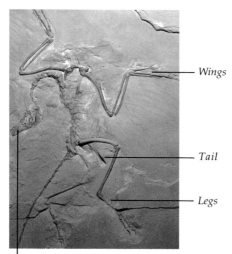

Wings

Tail

Legs

Teeth

EVOLUTIONARY EXPERIMENT

Although fossils show that pterosaurs were highly successful in their time, they all died out 65 million years ago. They were not directly related to the ancestors of modern birds.

AS DEAD AS THE DODO

The dodo, shown here in the famous fictional encounter with Lewis Carroll's heroine, Alice, in *Through the Looking-Glass*, was one of many birds whose end was caused by humans. The dodo was a flightless bird of Madagascar and neighboring islands in the Indian Ocean. It was driven to extinction in the late 17th century. Flying birds have also suffered at human hands. The last passenger pigeon died in 1914. One hundred years earlier, the species had formed flocks over a billion strong.

Front view of a crow's skeleton

STAYING BALANCED

Compared to many animals, birds are compact creatures. A bird's legs, wings, and neck are all lightweight structures. The heavy parts, especially its wing and leg muscles, are packed closely around the rib cage and backbone. This allows a bird to stay balanced both on the wing and on the ground.

Skull

Neck

Backbone

Wishbone

Coracoid bone

Rib cage

Leg bones

Eye socket

Nostril

Upper jawbone
of beak

Lower jawbone
of beak

Cranium (skull) made of
fused bones

Ear

THE STREAMLINED BODY
Although they differ in size, flying
birds like the crow have a
similar overall shape. This is
because they all need to be streamlined and cannot have structures that would mean
extra weight.

THE BIRD SKELETON
The evolution of powered flight has
left birds with skeletons that are
quite unlike those of other animals.
The most obvious feature in a flying
bird like the crow is its huge keel -
the projection from the breastbone
which anchors the wing muscles.
Birds do not have teeth, nor do they
have true tails; the tail feathers
are attached to a bony stump called
the pygostyle. The forelimbs are
completely adapted for use in
flight, and the toothless jaws have
evolved into a lightweight but very
strong beak that can be used for
preening feathers as well as
for feeding.

Back view of a
crow's skeleton

Skull

Neck

Backbone

Wing bones

Radius

Ulna

Pelvis

Pygostyle

Coracoid
bone

Wishbone, made up of
two joined collarbones,
helps to keep the
wing joint in
position as the
wing muscles
pull down-
ward

Keel, which anchors
the wing muscles
of flying birds

Backbone, made up of
small bones called
vertebrae, can bend where
the vertebrae are separated
but is rigid where they
are joined together

Humerus, an elongated wing
bone, corresponding to the
human upper arm bone

Radius, a wing bone,
corresponding to the
human lower arm bone

Ulna, a wing bone,
corresponding to the
human forearm bone

Hip girdle, or pelvis,
provides support for
the legs and an
area of bone for
the leg muscles
to attach to

Metacarpus

Thigh
bone
(femur)

Knee joint
(hidden by
feathers in
the living bird)

Lower leg
bone (tibia)

Claw (in living bird,
covered in horny
sheath)

Pygostyle - bony
stump to which
tail feathers are
attached

Ankle, or false knee -
although it may look
as if the knee bends
"back to front", this is
actually the bird's
ankle, not its knee

Tarsus

Hind toe

Birds as animals

As a group of animals, birds have evolved a staggering range of body sizes. The smallest living bird, the bee hummingbird, weighs only 0.05 oz (1.6 g) and is dwarfed by many butterflies and moths in its rain forest home. The largest bird, the North African ostrich, has been known to weigh up to 275 lb (125 kg) - making it nearly 80,000 times heavier than its tiny and distant relative. Between these two extremes are the great majority of the Earth's birds - an enormous variety of species that have managed to colonize habitats as different as polar ice, and tropical rain forests.

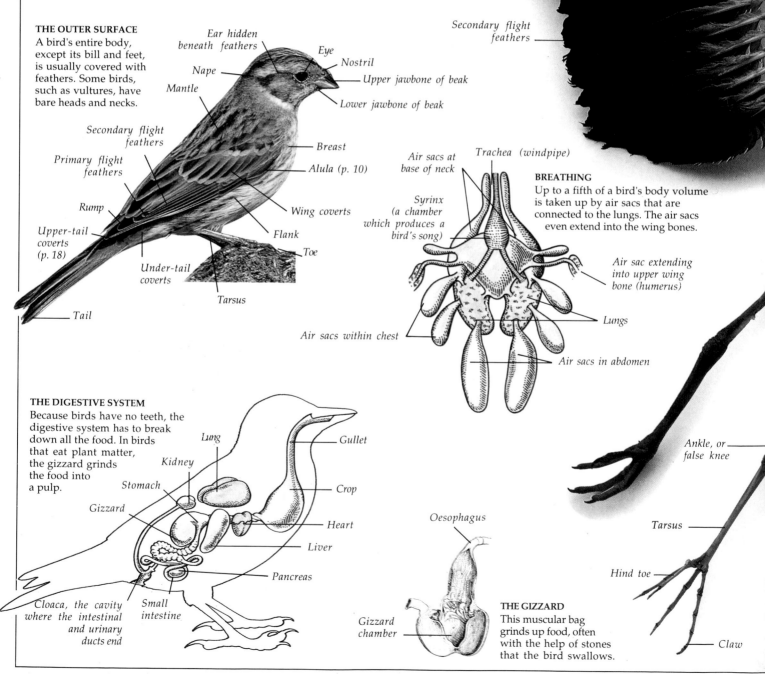

Primary flight feathers

Alula

Secondary flight feathers

THE OUTER SURFACE
A bird's entire body, except its bill and feet, is usually covered with feathers. Some birds, such as vultures, have bare heads and necks.

Ear hidden beneath feathers

Eye

Nostril

Nape

Upper jawbone of beak

Mantle

Lower jawbone of beak

Secondary flight feathers

Breast

Primary flight feathers

Alula (p. 10)

Rump

Wing coverts

Upper-tail coverts (p. 18)

Flank

Toe

Under-tail coverts

Tarsus

Tail

BREATHING
Up to a fifth of a bird's body volume is taken up by air sacs that are connected to the lungs. The air sacs even extend into the wing bones.

Air sacs at base of neck

Trachea (windpipe)

Syrinx (a chamber which produces a bird's song)

Air sac extending into upper wing bone (humerus)

Lungs

Air sacs within chest

Air sacs in abdomen

THE DIGESTIVE SYSTEM
Because birds have no teeth, the digestive system has to break down all the food. In birds that eat plant matter, the gizzard grinds the food into a pulp.

Lung

Gullet

Kidney

Stomach

Crop

Gizzard

Heart

Liver

Pancreas

Cloaca, the cavity where the intestinal and urinary ducts end

Small intestine

Oesophagus

Ankle, or false knee

Tarsus

Hind toe

Gizzard chamber

THE GIZZARD
This muscular bag grinds up food, often with the help of stones that the bird swallows.

Claw

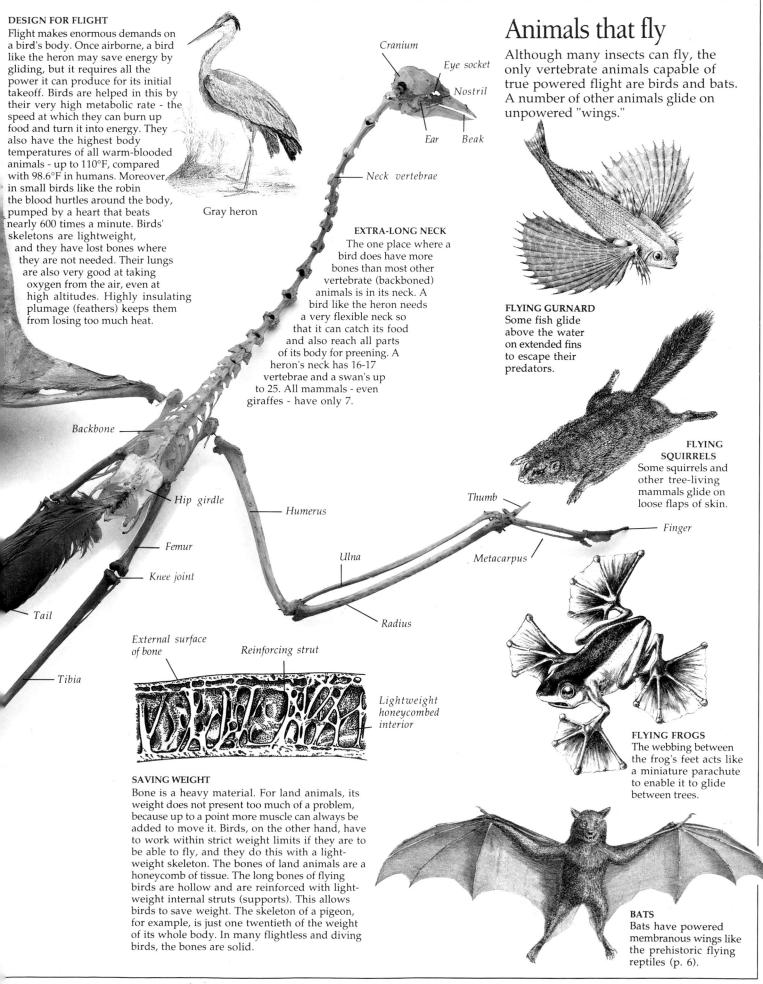

DESIGN FOR FLIGHT

Flight makes enormous demands on a bird's body. Once airborne, a bird like the heron may save energy by gliding, but it requires all the power it can produce for its initial takeoff. Birds are helped in this by their very high metabolic rate - the speed at which they can burn up food and turn it into energy. They also have the highest body temperatures of all warm-blooded animals - up to 110°F, compared with 98.6°F in humans. Moreover, in small birds like the robin the blood hurtles around the body, pumped by a heart that beats nearly 600 times a minute. Birds' skeletons are lightweight, and they have lost bones where they are not needed. Their lungs are also very good at taking oxygen from the air, even at high altitudes. Highly insulating plumage (feathers) keeps them from losing too much heat.

Gray heron

Cranium

Eye socket

Nostril

Ear *Beak*

Neck vertebrae

EXTRA-LONG NECK
The one place where a bird does have more bones than most other vertebrate (backboned) animals is in its neck. A bird like the heron needs a very flexible neck so that it can catch its food and also reach all parts of its body for preening. A heron's neck has 16-17 vertebrae and a swan's up to 25. All mammals - even giraffes - have only 7.

Animals that fly

Although many insects can fly, the only vertebrate animals capable of true powered flight are birds and bats. A number of other animals glide on unpowered "wings."

FLYING GURNARD
Some fish glide above the water on extended fins to escape their predators.

FLYING SQUIRRELS
Some squirrels and other tree-living mammals glide on loose flaps of skin.

Backbone

Hip girdle

Femur

Knee joint

Tail

Tibia

Humerus

Ulna

Radius

Thumb

Finger

Metacarpus

External surface of bone

Reinforcing strut

Lightweight honeycombed interior

SAVING WEIGHT
Bone is a heavy material. For land animals, its weight does not present too much of a problem, because up to a point more muscle can always be added to move it. Birds, on the other hand, have to work within strict weight limits if they are to be able to fly, and they do this with a light-weight skeleton. The bones of land animals are a honeycomb of tissue. The long bones of flying birds are hollow and are reinforced with light-weight internal struts (supports). This allows birds to save weight. The skeleton of a pigeon, for example, is just one twentieth of the weight of its whole body. In many flightless and diving birds, the bones are solid.

FLYING FROGS
The webbing between the frog's feet acts like a miniature parachute to enable it to glide between trees.

BATS
Bats have powered membranous wings like the prehistoric flying reptiles (p. 6).

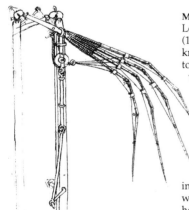

The wing

ONLY A FEW ANIMALS - insects, bats, and birds - are capable of powered flight. Of these three, birds are by far the largest, fastest, and most powerful fliers. The secret of their success lies in the design of their wings. A bird's wing is light, strong, and flexible. It is also slightly curved from front to back, producing an airfoil profile, like an airplane wing, that pulls the bird upward as it flaps through the air. Although the size and shape of wings vary according to a bird's individual lifestyle, all share the same pattern, shown here in the wing of an owl.

OVER THE LIMIT
A bird's wings can bear its weight, plus light luggage such as food and nesting materials. Heavier loads, like human passengers, are strictly out of the question.

FLIGHT OF FANCY
Legend has it that as Icarus flew from Crete to Greece, he climbed too near the sun and the wax that held his feathers melted. But birds flying at high altitudes have to cope with quite different and much more real problems - thin air, little oxygen, and intense cold.

ALULA
This group of feathers is held open in slow flight to prevent stalling.

MECHANICAL MIMICRY
Leonardo da Vinci (1452-1519) drew on his knowledge of bird wings to design machines that would imitate their flight. He replaced bones with wood, tendons with ropes, and feathers with sailcloth. As far as is known, none of these devices ever got beyond his drawing board. Anyway, they would have been far too heavy to fly.

FLAPPING FAILURES
The heroic birdmen of bygone days did not realize that flapping flight would always be beyond the power of human muscles. True man-powered flight has been achieved only through the later invention of the propeller.

PRIMARY FLIGHT FEATHERS
The "primaries" produce the power for flight as the bird brings its wings downward. The outermost primaries can be used for steering, like the flaps on a plane's wing.

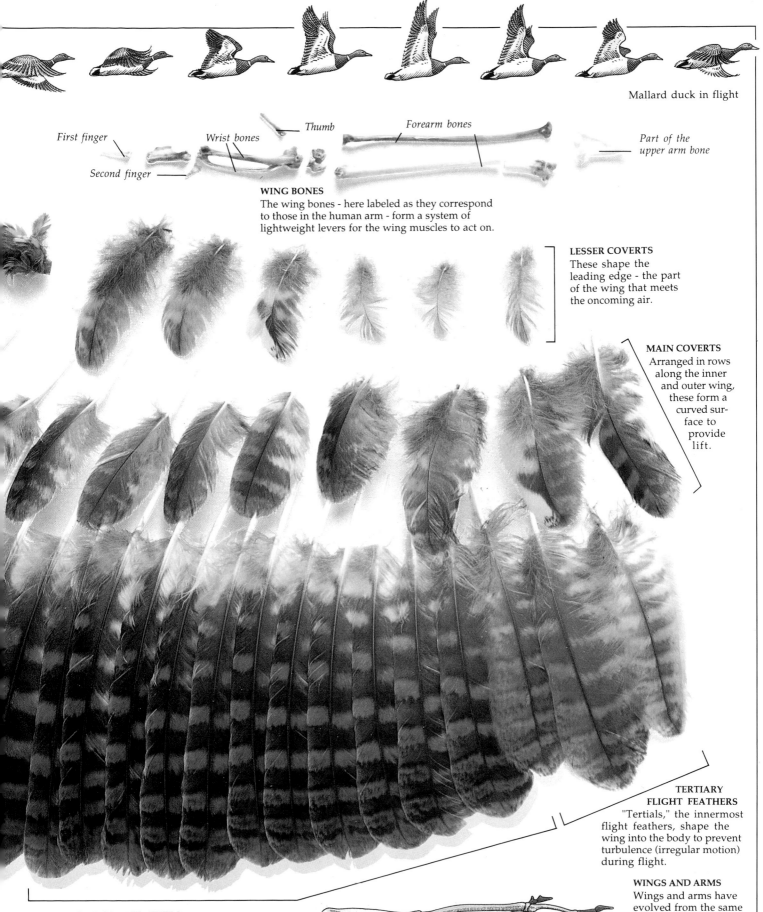

Mallard duck in flight

WING BONES

First finger

Second finger

Wrist bones

Thumb

Forearm bones

Part of the upper arm bone

The wing bones - here labeled as they correspond to those in the human arm - form a system of lightweight levers for the wing muscles to act on.

LESSER COVERTS
These shape the leading edge - the part of the wing that meets the oncoming air.

MAIN COVERTS
Arranged in rows along the inner and outer wing, these form a curved surface to provide lift.

TERTIARY FLIGHT FEATHERS
"Tertials," the innermost flight feathers, shape the wing into the body to prevent turbulence (irregular motion) during flight.

WINGS AND ARMS
Wings and arms have evolved from the same type of limb. However, the wing has only three digits, and some of the wrist bones are fused together. Here corresponding bones are colored the same.

SECONDARY FLIGHT FEATHERS
On the inner wing, the "secondaries" form the curve that provides lift.

Bones of a bird's wing

Bones of a human arm

Maneuverability and fast takeoff

FOR MANY BIRDS, being able to pursue prey or escape enemies over quite short distances is much more important than being able to stay in the air for a long time. A broad, rounded wing is best for this type of flight, because it gives good acceleration (speed) and can be adjusted for steering. This type of wing is particularly common in woodland birds like woodpeckers and grouse, and birds that live on the ground, such as finches.

OWL FLIGHT
The barn owl has a slow, buoyant flight.

Greenfinch wing

FINCH FLIGHT
Finches shut their wings periodically to save energy.

Broad wingtip

QUICK ON THE TURN
The greenfinch's blunt, rounded wing shape is typical of finches. Except when migrating, finches rarely fly far. They constantly veer and turn on the wing. A flock of finches will burst into the air at the least sign of danger.

Greenfinch

Primary flight feathers are curved and broad

Fringed feather edges reduce air disturbance and cut down the noise produced by flight

Owl wing coverts have a soft, downy texture

Barn owl

MUFFLED WINGS
A barn owl's wing is almost furry to the touch. Its fringed feathers muffle the wingbeats so that small animals do not hear the owl's approach.

Barn owl wing

Roller wing

Broad flight feathers for maneuverability

Roller

PERCH TO PERCH
The roller, a bird about the size of a jay, catches small animals by swooping down onto them. It spots its prey from its perches on walls and trees and moves between perches with a slow, almost leisurely flight.

Light and dark bars camouflage bird when feeding on ground

Wing has a broad surface for maneuverability but a pointed tip for speed

READY TO ESCAPE
Most doves and pigeons are hunted by many enemies, including humans. Strong wing muscles (making up a third of its weight) enable them to take off rapidly and accelerate to 50 mph (80 kph).

Crested pigeon wing

ROLLER FLIGHT
The roller has a heavy up-and-down flight.

TURTLE DOVE FLIGHT
The wings beat rapidly without pauses.

Turtle dove

Woodpecker wing

*Green
coloring
for
camouflage*

WOODPECKER FLIGHT
Woodpeckers climb and
dive much more steeply
than most other birds.

Pheasants in flight

Pheasant wing

*Folded
flight feathers*

STEERING A SAFE COURSE
In dense forests, a green woodpecker needs short, rounded wings
so that it can turn suddenly to avoid
obstacles. Its wing shape also helps
it come to a controlled landing when
approaching a tree.

Woodpecker

*Camouflaged inner
wing feathers conceal
bird on ground*

*Camouflaged plumage
found only on the
female*

**VERTICAL
TAKEOFF**
Pheasants are
reluctant fliers. If
alarmed, they take off
almost vertically on
their broad wings. Once
airborne, they then
glide away in a
straight line.

FLYING FOR COVER
Grouse, like pheasants
and other game birds,
spend most of their
time on the ground. On
sensing danger, they
first crouch down. Then
- waiting almost till
the last moment - they
spring upward, at the
same time bringing
their opened wings
sharply downward, to
burst into the air.
Grouse fly by
alternating rapid
wingbeats with short
glides and only cover a
short distance before
landing. In nearly all
game birds, the
female's wings are
camouflaged
and the
male's are
more not-
iceable.

PHEASANT FLIGHT
Rapid wingbeats
are followed by a
long glide.

Female
black grouse
or "blackhen"

Female black grouse
or "blackhen" wing

*Long flight feathers
allow the grouse
to glide*

Male black grouse or "blackcock" wing

13

Speed and endurance

WHEN A SWIFT makes its first brief landing before nesting, it brings to an end a flight that may have lasted nonstop for three years. The swift is just one of a number of birds that land only to breed, and its slender, curved wings are completely adapted for continuous use. In a similar way, the wings of all other birds have evolved for a particular kind of flight. In general, birds that fly rapidly and powerfully, like the swift, have pointed wings. This wing shape provides the bird with enough lift without producing too much drag - the friction against the air which tends to slow a bird down.

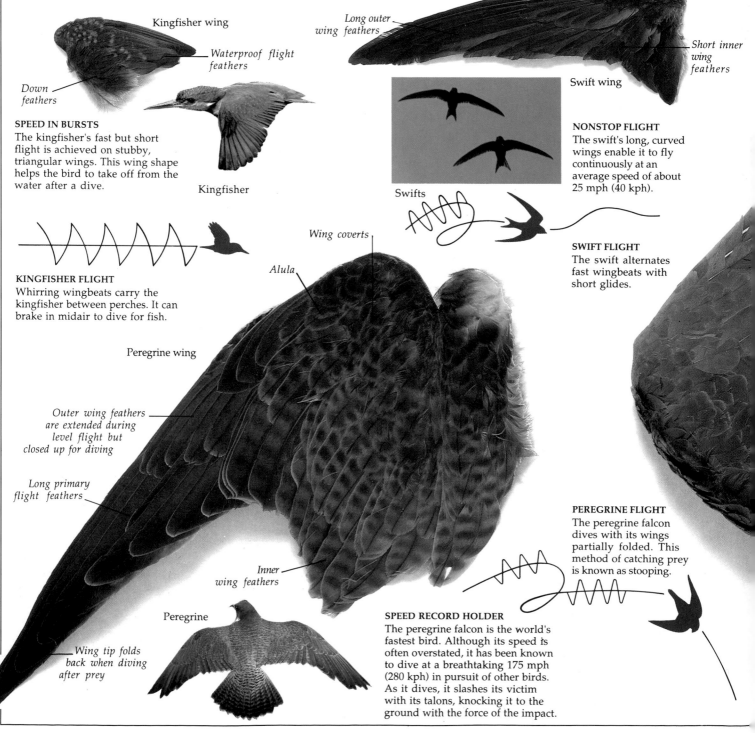

Kingfisher wing

Waterproof flight feathers

Down feathers

SPEED IN BURSTS
The kingfisher's fast but short flight is achieved on stubby, triangular wings. This wing shape helps the bird to take off from the water after a dive.

Kingfisher

Long outer wing feathers

Short inner wing feathers

Swift wing

NONSTOP FLIGHT
The swift's long, curved wings enable it to fly continuously at an average speed of about 25 mph (40 kph).

Swifts

KINGFISHER FLIGHT
Whirring wingbeats carry the kingfisher between perches. It can brake in midair to dive for fish.

Wing coverts

Alula

SWIFT FLIGHT
The swift alternates fast wingbeats with short glides.

Peregrine wing

Outer wing feathers are extended during level flight but closed up for diving

Long primary flight feathers

Inner wing feathers

Peregrine

Wing tip folds back when diving after prey

PEREGRINE FLIGHT
The peregrine falcon dives with its wings partially folded. This method of catching prey is known as stooping.

SPEED RECORD HOLDER
The peregrine falcon is the world's fastest bird. Although its speed is often overstated, it has been known to dive at a breathtaking 175 mph (280 kph) in pursuit of other birds. As it dives, it slashes its victim with its talons, knocking it to the ground with the force of the impact.

LONG-HAUL MIGRANTS

Many geese travel enormous distances each year to breed in the Arctic tundra. Their flight is not particularly fast - they cruise at about 35 mph (55 kph) - but they are able to maintain this speed for many hours without stopping. Snow geese, for example, have been known to travel 1,700 miles (2,700 km) in two and a half days. Goose wings are long and broad to provide the lift needed to keep birds weighing up to 11 lb (5 kg) airborne.

Lesser white-fronted goose

Shoveler wing

Inner wing coverts

Primary flight feathers

Speculum exposed during flight

RAPID TRANSIT

Ducks like the shoveler migrate to breed, but their journeys are usually shorter than those of geese and their flight faster. A migrating duck can travel up to 1,000 miles (1,600 km) in a single day, averaging nearly 40 mph (70 kph). Many ducks have a brightly colored patch, speculum, on each wing, and others only develop them during the breeding season.

Shoveler

Strong primary flight feathers

WATERFOWL FLIGHT

Both ducks and geese beat their wings constantly during flight.

Primary flight feathers

Speculum

Pointed tip of folded wing

Pintail wing

WATERPROOF WINGS

The pintail, like most ducks, can escape from danger with a twisting and turning flight. It opens and closes its pointed wings to help it change direction. To keep its wings airworthy, the pintail waterproofs them with oil produced by a gland on its back and carefully preens them so that they lie in their correct position.

Pintail

Broad wing surface gives maximum lift for takeoff and long-distance flight

Lesser white-fronted goose wing

Soaring, gliding, and hovering

WHEN A BIRD FLAPS ITS WINGS, it uses up a great deal of energy - about 15 times as much as when it is sitting still. But some birds have managed to evolve ways of flying that take much less effort than this. Large birds do it by soaring and gliding - harnessing the power of the sun or the wind to keep them in the air. Right at the other extreme is hovering - keeping still in the air by beating the wings nonstop, just as a swimmer treads water to stay afloat.

Hummingbirds, the smallest flying birds, hover while feeding

Narrow wing provides lift without too much drag during gliding

Great black-backed gull wing

GLIDING GULLS
Slender, pointed wings enable gulls to glide on updrafts - currents of air forced upward by cliffs and hillsides. The lift generated by these updrafts is enough to support birds as heavy as the great black-backed gull, which weighs over 4.5 lb (2 kg).

Great black-backed gull

GULL FLIGHT
In flapping flight, a gull may travel at 25 mph (40 kph), but in a strong updraft, it can stay motionless over the ground.

Inner wing coverts mould wing to the body

"Slotted" primary flight feathers reduce disturbances

Kestrel wing

HANGING IN THE AIR
Although many birds can hover momentarily, few can keep up this type of flight, as it is very tiring. One exception is the kestrel, which hovers as its keen eyes pinpoint small animals from high overhead. It needs a slight head wind to help keep it up.

Kestrel

KESTREL FLIGHT
The kestrel has the fluttering forward flight typical of falcons.

KESTREL HOVERING
The wings beat rapidly and the tail is fanned out to provide lift as the wind blows past.

Birds that cannot fly

Millions of years ago, giant flightless birds roamed the Earth. Today only a few dozen smaller species survive.

Penguin flipper

Stiff wing blade acts as a propeller

Densely packed feathers

Rhea wing

WINGS AS FLIPPERS
Penguins swim by "flying" under-water with their wings. One species, the emperor penguin, can dive up to 800 ft (250 m) using its wings to move forward. Penguins' wings cannot be folded up like those of most birds.

Adelie penguins in Antarctica

Rhea

Inner wing

THE HEAVIEST BIRD
Ornithologists - scientists who study birds - calculate that no bird heavier than 40 lb (18 kg) can fly. Above that weight, muscle power would never be enough to keep a bird airborne. The African ostrich, weighing in at 260 lb (120 kg), is nearly seven times over this limit. Its wings are no more than weak flaps with a fan of 16 fluffy flight feathers. Although the ostrich cannot fly, it can run at speeds of over 30 mph (50 kph) and over-take many flying birds.

Downy feathers provide insulation but cannot produce lift

PAMPAS RUNNER
Rheas are the South American counterparts of ostriches. Their wing feathers are long, but useless for flight.

Outer wing

Straight leading edge is held slanting upward during soaring

Primary flight feathers are used for maneuvering

Splayed (extended) "fingers" help to reduce air disturbances

Broad inner flight feathers provide lift as bird soars within a thermal

Buzzard wing

UP WITHOUT EFFORT
Heavy birds of prey like the buzzard soar on thermals - columns of warm, rising air. They need flapping flight only to get from one thermal to the next.

Buzzard

BUZZARD FLIGHT
All soaring birds bank (turn) tightly to keep within the rising air of a thermal.

Tails

DURING the course of evolution, birds have gradually lost the part of the backbone that in other animals makes up the tail, and have replaced it with feathers. The size of these feathers differs from bird to bird. Some birds like murres and puffins hardly have any tail at all. Others like peacocks and male birds of paradise have tails that are so long they make flight quite difficult.

RUMP FEATHERS
Above the base of a wood pigeon's tail, the rump feathers provide insulation with their thick down.

Wood pigeon

TAIL COVERTS
Dense rows of these feathers lie over the base of the bird's tail and smooth the airflow over it.

Tail fanned on approach; body held horizontally

Landing; feet held forward to grasp perch

Tail closed as bird settles on perch

AIR BRAKE
When a bird comes in to land, it lowers and spreads out its tail feathers. The feathers act as a brake and slow the bird's approach.

TAIL FEATHERS
The wood pigeon, like most birds, has 12 tail feathers. The feather tips get frayed by the wear and tear of flight.

Tips worn and frayed by flight

Tail shapes

Flight puts many restrictions on a bird's shape. For this reason, birds that spend much of their time flying almost always have lightweight, streamlined tails. But other birds, especially those that live on the ground or in forests, have evolved tails that are shaped for uses other than flight. Some of these are used for balance, some for perching, and others for attracting the attention of a mate.

Rump feathers

Tail coverts

Rump feathers showing distinctive orange coloration, revealed during flight

Tail coverts

Crossbill tail

Tail coverts

Fork to aid maneuverability

FORKED TAILS

In some birds, the central tail feathers are the longest. In others, particularly many of the finches, the situation is reversed and the tail has a forked shape. This arrangement probably gives small birds greater ability to maneuver.

Crossbill

Magpie

A TAIL FOR BALANCE

The central feathers in a magpie's tail are nearly 10 in (25 cm) long. Long tails are normally used for display (pp. 28-29), but because both male and female magpies have them, it is more likely that they are used for balancing on the ground or clambering in trees.

Elongated tail feathers

Magpie tail

Downy black-tipped rump feathers lying above tail coverts

Green woodpecker tail

Rump feathers

Great spotted woodpecker

Rump feathers

Tail coverts

Tail coverts

Curved tail feathers used in display by male

Tail coverts

Stiff quills

Sharp points created by rubbing of tail against trees

Great spotted woodpecker

Black grouse tail

TAILS FOR SUPPORT

A woodpecker uses its tail to brace itself as it climbs the trunk of a tree. Woodpecker tail feathers are unusually stiff so that they can support a large amount of the bird's weight. Being subjected to rather rough treatment, the tips of the feathers rapidly wear down.

Male pheasant with wing and tail feathers revealed during takeoff

A TAIL FOR DISPLAY

In the black grouse, the male's tail feathers are crescent shaped, and the female's are straight. Differences like this are a sure sign that the tail has evolved this shape for display rather than for flight.

Black grouse

Peacock

The structure of feathers

FEATHERS are the great evolutionary development that separates birds from all other animals. A humming-bird's plumage may number under 1,000 feathers; and a large bird like the swan may have over 25,000, with nearly four fifths of these covering the head and neck alone. Like hair, claws, and horns, feathers are made from a protein called keratin. It is this substance that gives them their great strength and flexibility. But for all their complex structure, fully grown feathers are quite dead. As feathers develop, they split apart to form a mesh of filaments that link together. Once this has happened, their blood supply is cut off. The feathers then serve their time, unless lost by accident, and when worn out they are finally discarded during molting.

BREAKABLE PLUMAGE
A Central American motmot changes the shape of its tail feathers during preening. When it pecks at a tail feather, the feather's barbs break off to leave a bare shaft ending in a spoon-shaped tip. Why it does this has not yet been discovered.

Feather sheaths

Emerging feather tufts

Growing feathers within sheaths

HOW FEATHERS GROW
Feathers start their growth as pulp inside tubes known as feather sheaths. The tip of a feather gradually emerges from the growing sheath, unrolling and splitting apart to form a flat blade. Eventually the feather sheath falls away, leaving the fully formed feather.

FEATHER SHAFT
The hollow shaft contains the dried remains of the pulp.

Hollow interior

Pulp from interior of shaft

Fully grown feathers after the protective sheaths have fallen away

Quill tip embedded in skin and attached to muscles

PEOPLE AND FEATHERS
Feathers have long been used by people for decoration and for more practical purposes. Headdresses and quill pens made use of flight feathers. The down feathers of ducks and geese are still used for bedding, and the brilliantly colored plumes of some trop-ical birds find their way into objects such as fishing flies.

Quill

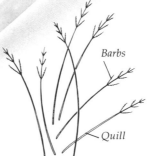

Barbs

Quill

FILOPLUMES
These hairlike growths, found between the feathers on a bird's body, help a bird to detect how its feathers are lying.

Aftershaft second shaft from a single quill

SPLIT FEATHERS
Some feathers are split to form two different halves attached to the same shaft. This enables a single feather to perform two different functions.

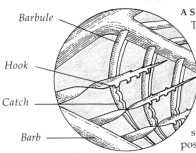

Barbule

Hook

Catch

Barb

A SURFACE FOR FLIGHT
To work effectively, a flight feather has to form a single continuous surface for air to flow over. This surface is produced by thousands of barbules. These lie on either side of each barb and lock together as hooks and catches. If barbule hooks come loose, a bird simply preens them back into position with its beak.

Feather tip

Notch for reducing air disturbance (p. 24)

Outer vane (faces into the wind)

Rachis, or shaft

Downcurved edge

Upcurved edge

Inner vane (faces away from the wind)

Parallel barbs locked together to form a smooth surface

Magnification of macaw feather showing barbs and barbules

FEATHERS WITHIN FEATHERS
Under high magnification, barbs and barbules look almost like miniature feathers. On flight feathers like this, the barbs are closely packed and the barbules are short and numerous. By contrast, on down feathers there are fewer barbs but they are much longer. It is not unusual for them to have no barbules at all (p. 26).

Only the parallel barbs are visible in this magnification of a scarlet macaw's flight feather

Feather care

Feathers receive a tremendous battering during daily use. They also become dirty and infested with parasites such as feather lice. Most feathers are shed every year during molting, but birds still spend a lot of time making sure their plumage stays in a good condition. They do this by preening - using the beak like a comb to draw together the barbs and barbules - and also by special methods of feather care, such as oiling, powdering, and bathing, both in water and in dust.

POWDERED PLUMAGE
Egrets, herons, and some other birds have special feathers that break up to form a powder. This "powder down" is used to keep the plumage in good condition. Unlike other feathers, powder down feathers never stop growing.

ANTING JAYS
Jays sometimes encourage ants to swarm over their feathers. Poisonous formic acid produced by the ants may drive out parasites in the jay's plumage.

DUST BATHS
Dust both absorbs and scrapes things away. Bathing in dust scours dirt from a bird's feathers.

Feathers

THE FEATHERS that make up a bird's plumage are of four main types: down feathers, body feathers, tail feathers, and wing feathers. Although many of them are drab and dull, others are beautifully shaped and colored structures.

DOWN FEATHERS
Soft, finely divided feathers trap a layer of air to provide insulation.

Peacock

Pigeon

BODY FEATHERS
The feathers that streamline a bird's body.

Macaw

African gray parrot

Red lory

Parrots

Macaws

TAIL FEATHERS
Feathers for steering, balance, and display.

Goose

Goose

Flamingo

Peacock

Pheasants

Peacock

Palawan

Golden pheasant

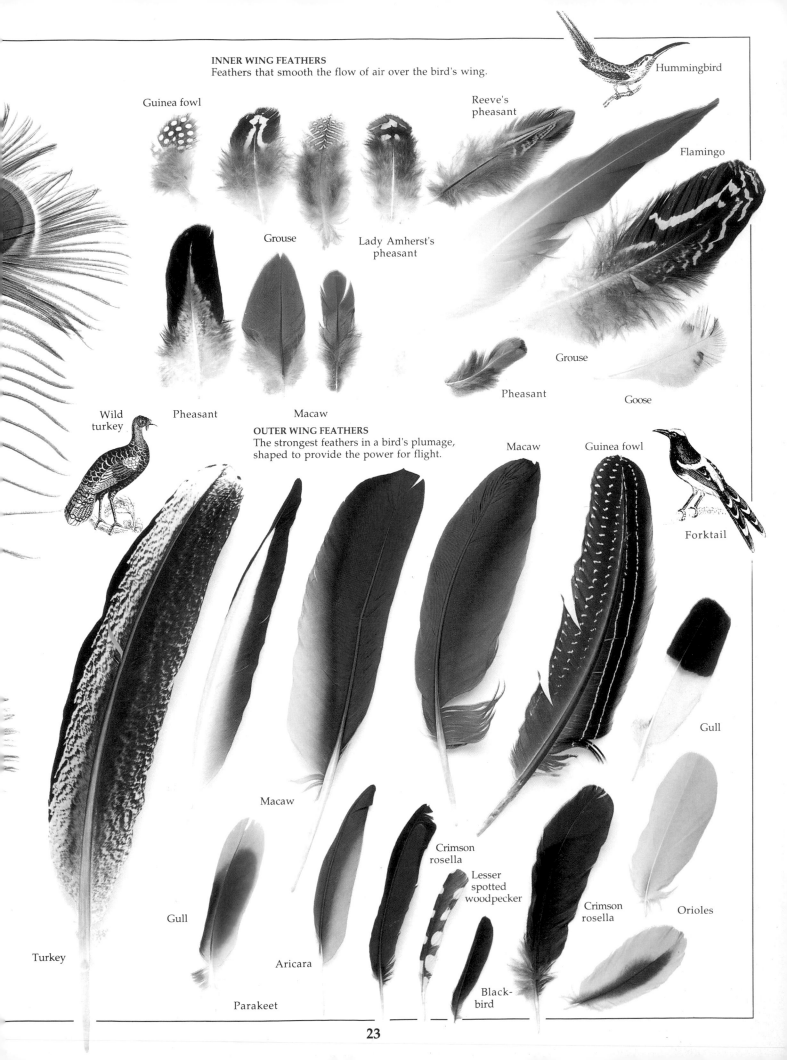

INNER WING FEATHERS
Feathers that smooth the flow of air over the bird's wing.

Hummingbird

Guinea fowl

Reeve's pheasant

Flamingo

Grouse

Lady Amherst's pheasant

Grouse

Pheasant

Goose

Wild turkey

Pheasant

Macaw

OUTER WING FEATHERS
The strongest feathers in a bird's plumage, shaped to provide the power for flight.

Macaw

Guinea fowl

Forktail

Gull

Macaw

Crimson rosella

Lesser spotted woodpecker

Crimson rosella

Orioles

Gull

Aricara

Turkey

Parakeet

Blackbird

Wing feathers

THE WING FEATHERS are one of the most important parts of a bird's flying machinery. They combine strength with lightness and flexibility. Compared with the rest of the body, the wings have relatively few feathers, but each one is important, working with its neighbors to form a perfect surface for flight.

The outer wing

The long feathers of the outer wing provide most of the bird's flight power and keep it from stalling. The outermost flight feathers help a bird to steer by spreading open or closing up in flight.

Barn owl
Green woodpecker
Jay

Adult starling
Young starling

OUTER COVERTS
By overlapping the bases of the flight feathers, the coverts smooth the flow of air.

LOPSIDED DESIGN
Nearly all flight feathers are like this cockateel's - narrower on their leading edge. This design produces lift as the feather slices through the air.

GRADED SHAPES
Away from the wing-tip, the flight feathers become gradually shorter and broader. These are from a regent parrot.

Fringe

Wider trailing edge

Slot

Narrow leading edge

Tawny owl
Barn owl

HEAVY-DUTY FEATHERS
The mute swan, which weighs up to 26 lb (12 kg), needs especially long and strong feathers to power its flight. Its outer wing feathers can be up to 18 in (45 cm) long but even so, each feather weighs only 0.5 oz (14 g).

ABOVE AND BELOW
Many wing feathers are different colors underneath. Macaws' feathers bend light to produce shimmery colors - in this species blue above and yellow below.

SILENT FEATHERS
Fringes on the edges of owl feathers break up the flow of air and silence the owl's flight, as shown on this tawny owl feather.

SLOTTED FEATHERS
The deep slot in this crow feather forms a gap in the wing that reduces irregular motion.

Swan

The inner wing

Inner wing feathers are generally shorter than those on the outer wing. They are not subject to so much force during flight and, for this reason, their quills are shorter and the feathers are less well anchored. With the exception of some display feathers, they are also more evenly shaped than outer wing feathers.

A BALANCED BLADE
Inner wing feathers, here the regent parrot's, point away from the wind, not across it. They therefore do not need a lopsided shape to provide lift like the outer wing feathers.

IN-FLIGHT MARKINGS
The bright colors of many birds, such as budgerigars, are revealed only when the wings are fully open.

THE MANDARIN DUCK'S SAIL
The male mandarin duck has a pair of these extraordinary sail feathers - one at the base of each wing. They are shown off during courtship.

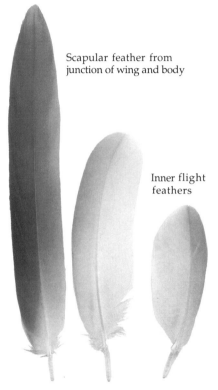

Scapular feather from junction of wing and body

Inner flight feathers

Curlew   Mallard   Jay

AT THE BOUNDARY
Flight feathers at the boundary between the inner and outer wing have curved quills and blunt tips. They may have bright patterns that show up in flight.

CAMOUFLAGED FEATHERS
Patterned brown feathers hide the woodcock from enemies (p. 30).

COLORED BY ITS DIET
The flamingo's striking pink color is determined by the bird's natural diet of plankton, diatoms, and blue-green algae, which initiates a complex pigment process.

Bustard

Rook

Eagle owl

Curlew

UNDERWING FEATHERS
Like the upperwing coverts, these lie close together to smooth the flow of air. Their surface is concave (curved in), rather than convex (curved out) as in the upper wing.

INFREQUENT FLIERS
This feather is from a wild turkey. Like many birds that live on the ground, it rarely uses its feathers for flight.

INNER COVERTS
The inner coverts, in this case from a buzzard, overlap the front feathers of the inner wing. Their down shows that they are also used for insulating the body when the wing is folded.

Body, down, and tail feathers

FEATHERS are not only designed for flight. They also insulate and water-proof a bird's body and enable it to conceal itself, attract a mate, incubate its eggs, and stay balanced when on the ground. All these tasks are performed by three types of feathers: body feathers, down feathers, and the feathers in the tail. The way these feathers work depends on their shape and whether or not their barbs can lock together.

Down feathers

Down feathers are found next to the bird's skin. Their barbs do not lock together but instead spread out to form a soft, irregular mass. Down is one of the most effective insulating materials found in the animal kingdom.

Barb
Quill

UNLOCKED BARBS
In this peacock down feather, the separate barbs can be seen. These barbs trap air, which forms an insulation layer below the body feathers.

THERMAL CLADDING
Small down feathers like this one from a partridge are packed together tightly on the bird's body to form a furlike mat.

FEATHERS FOR INCUBATION
Many birds, including the teal, pull out breast feathers to insulate their eggs. Some are collected and sold for bedding.

DUAL-FUNCTION FEATHER
Many feathers have a mass of down near the point where they are attached to the body, as shown on this silver pheasant feather.

Body feathers

Body feathers come in a huge range of shapes and sizes. Some are used just to insulate and cover the bird's body, but others have developed for display (pp. 28-29) and have evolved bright colors or strange shapes.

Red lory feathers

African gray parrot feathers

Macaw feathers

PATTERNS ON THE SURFACE
In many boldly patterned birds, only the exposed tips of the feathers show distinctive markings - the rest of the feather is dull, as on this pheasant.

TROPICAL BRILLIANCE
Brilliant and varied body colors are more common in birds that live in the tropics than those that live in moderate regions. Bright colors may help birds to identify their own kind among the many others that share their habitat.

Long quill

COURTSHIP PLUMES
Some birds have evolved body feathers that are completely adapted for a role in attracting a mate. These hanging feathers adorn the neck of the male wild turkey. Each feather is divided into a pair of plumes.

FLYING HEAVYWEIGHT
This body feather comes from a bustard, one of the world's heaviest flying birds.

LEAFY CAMOUFLAGE
The dull green tips of the green woodpecker's body feathers are ideal camouflage against the woodland leaves of its natural habitat.

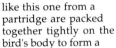
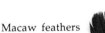

A PHEASANT'S CAPE
The neck feathers of the male golden pheasant form a brilliant black-and-gold cape. These feathers were once highly prized by fishermen for use in fishing flies.

Shortened barbs

Tail feathers

Birds use their tails for three things - to steer them during flight, to balance when perched or on the ground, and to impress a mate or a rival during courtship. Because of this, tail feathers come in a great range of shapes, sizes and colors, something that is especially noticeable in breeding male birds.

A CURLED TAIL
The male mallard has two distinctive curled feathers at the base of his tail. When he courts a mate, he throws his head up and shows off his plumage. The female's tail feathers are straight.

EYED FEATHERS
The "eyes" on the peacock's tail extend right down to the short feathers at the tail's base, making a spectacular courtship display.

Growing feather

Mature feather

Feather sheath

— Quill

STRESS BARS
The light-colored bars in this parrot's tail feather are caused by changes in diet that occurred during the feather's growth.

BRED FOR COLOR
Varied colors in budgerigars are the result of controlled breeding. Wild budgerigars are blue and green; other colors are found only in birds bred under control.

YOUNG AND OLD
Here, a growing tail feather from a kestrel is shown alongside a fully grown one. Both feathers are from a bird molting into adult plumage.

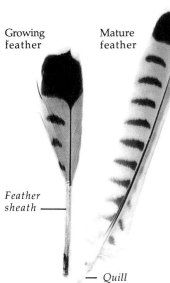

THE TAIL'S SIDES
The feathers that are farthest from the center of the tail are the least evenly shaped because, when the tail is fanned in the air, the outer feathers must provide lift when air blows across them. These lopsided tail feathers are from a curlew.

CENTRAL TAIL FEATHER
This even owl feather comes from the center of the tail.

IRIDESCENT TAILS
Magpies have long tail feathers that look black from a distance but seem colored when seen from nearby. As in the macaw's flight feathers (p. 24), this effect is caused by the bending of light.

GAME BIRD TAILS
The tails of male pheasants, chickens, and other game birds can be exceptionally long. Even this long feather from a pheasant's tail would be dwarfed by that of a Japanese red jungle fowl: its tail feathers have been bred to reach 35 ft (10.7 m).

Pheasant

Count Raggi's
bird of
paradise

Courtship

THE WAYS IN WHICH BIRDS FIND PARTNERS and mate is one of the most
fascinating and colorful features of all animal life. Although divorce
may be rare in birds, almost every other imaginable marriage
arrangement exists somewhere in the bird world. Having fought off
other males, often by establishing a territory, some males attract a
single mate and remain faithful to her for life. At the other extreme,
some males use their brilliant courtship plumage to attract a whole
series of mates, deserting each one in favor of the next as soon as
mating has taken place. Birds attract their mates by a combination
of visible signals that range from special plumage to brightly
colored legs and inflatable pouches. They also use ritual
movements that can be as simple as a gull's nod of
the head or as bizarre as the display of the male
great bustard, who throws
back his wings and
head and looks like he's
turning his head
inside out.

ROLE REVERSAL
Unusually for a bird,
the female red-necked
phalarope courts the
male. She is the more
brightly colored of
the two birds.

THE PEACOCK'S TAIL
Peacocks are members of the
pheasant family, a group of birds
that show some of the most spectacular and elaborate courtship
plumage in the bird world.

HIDDEN SUPPORT
From the back, the upright feathers
of the peacock's "true" tail can be
seen. These brace the much longer
and more brilliant tail
coverts.

ON PARADE
Male lyrebirds make
themselves arenas on
which they strut and
display. Their
movements attract a
series of mates.

Feathers without
barbules (p. 21) do not
interlock, so appear
lacy

Tip of quill

A MYSTERY SOLVED

It was only in the last century that naturalists explored the forests of New Guinea and saw how plumes like this from a Count Raggi's bird of paradise were used by male birds. In displays, during which they hang upside down, the birds throw their plumes open.

Body feathers

Streaked central feather

INFLATABLE ATTRACTION

The male frigate bird has a stunning red throat pouch that he uses to attract a mate. He keeps his pouch inflated for many hours until a female, lured by this irresistible courtship device, joins him.

DEFUSING TENSION

Although boobies and gannets nest in densely packed colonies, each bird will stab at any neighbor who dares to intrude on its small but very private "patch." When pairs meet, courtship ceremonies are needed to reduce these aggressive instincts. Here two blue-footed boobies join in the "pelican" display, pointing their beaks out of each other's way.

During display, these feathers are thrown open to produce a fountain of color as the male bird swings upside down from a branch

IN STEP WITH THE SEASON

The brilliant colors on puffins' beaks are at their brightest during the breeding season in early summer. The color lies in a horny sheath that covers the outside of the beak. When the puffins abandon their cliff-top burrows and head out to sea for the winter, this sheath falls off. The beak is then a much duller color until the following spring.

DANCING ON WATER

Great crested grebes perform a sequence of bizarre dances during their courtship. The sequence often begins with a head-shaking dance, in which the birds face each other, jerking their heads from side to side, as if trying to avoid each other's glance. Suddenly, they dive and reappear at the surface with beakfuls of waterweed. During the "penguin dance," both birds rear up out of the water, paddling furiously as they present the weed to each other. After several more dances, the birds mate.

MINIATURE RIVALS

Male hummingbirds, though tiny, aggressively defend their territories.

Camouflage

IN THE NATURAL WORLD, swaying reeds, beach pebbles, dead branches, and patches of snow are not always what they seem. Any one of them can suddenly burst into life to reveal its true identity - a bird that only moments before was perfectly camouflaged against its background. When faced with danger, most birds immediately take to the air. But some, especially those that feed or roost on the ground, prefer to take a chance that they will be overlooked. The birds that lie low the longest are those with camouflaged plumage. In these, the color and patterning of the feathers matches a particular kind of background, such as the forest floor.

Woodcock

HIDDEN AMONG THE PEBBLES
An open beach may seem a difficult place for a bird to conceal itself. But the moment it stops moving, a ringed plover vanishes among the beach pebbles.

Ringed plover

THE FIRST LINE OF DEFENSE
The woodcock is a forest bird that hunts mostly at night. Between dusk and dawn it probes the woodland floor for worms and other small animals, but during the day it roosts on the ground. If its camouflage fails to conceal it, the woodcock will take off and dash through the tree trunks with a swerving flight.

Probing beak

Seasonal changes

On high mountainsides, the winter snow completely changes the color of the landscape. Birds that do not fly south for the winter need some way to hide from their enemies. A few, like the rock ptarmigan (a type of grouse), do this by changing color. Because birds molt their feathers every year, they can change their color by shedding one set of feathers and replacing it with another, differently colored set. This enables them to camouflage themselves. In places where the snow never melts, birds like the snowy owl have white plumage all year long.

Rock ptarmigan in winter plumage

Rock ptarmigan in summer plumage

SEASONAL PLUMAGE
In summer, the rock ptarmigan's feathers are brown, enabling it to camouflage itself against rocks. But in the winter its plumage changes to white, thus concealing it effectively against snow.

Nightjar

A DAYTIME HIDEOUT
The nightjar is an insect eater that feeds only at dusk. By day it stays completely still, looking like a broken branch. There are records of resting nightjars being stepped on by walkers who did not notice birds right beneath their feet!

Feet and tracks

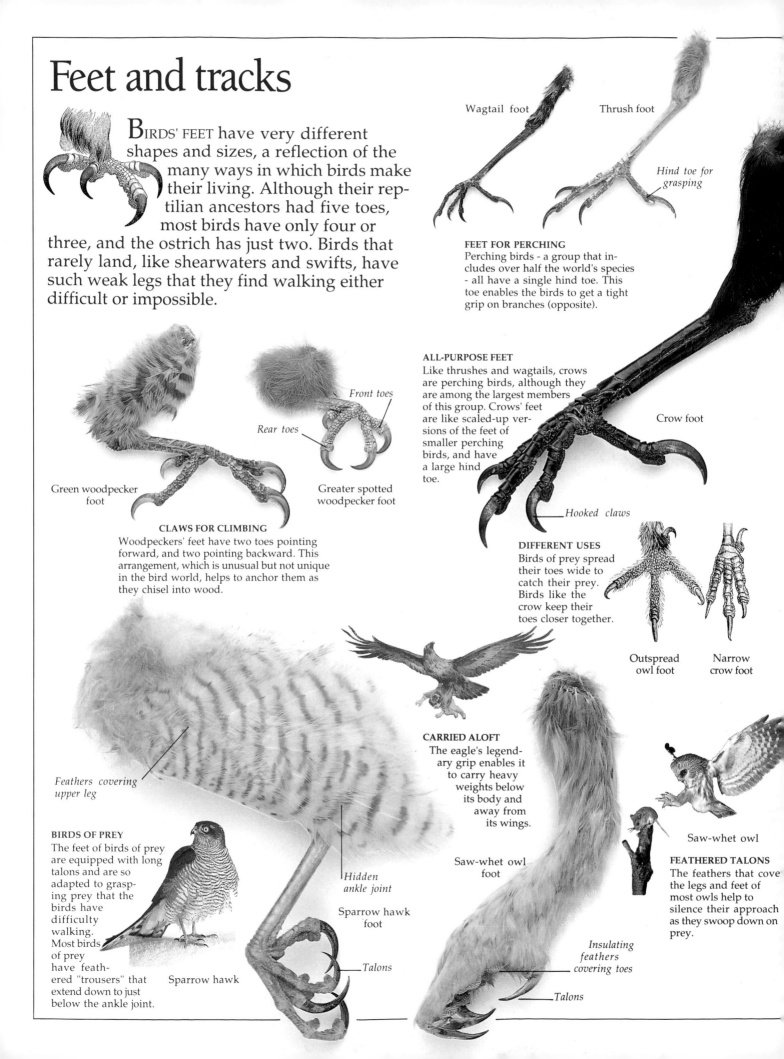

BIRDS' FEET have very different shapes and sizes, a reflection of the many ways in which birds make their living. Although their reptilian ancestors had five toes, most birds have only four or three, and the ostrich has just two. Birds that rarely land, like shearwaters and swifts, have such weak legs that they find walking either difficult or impossible.

Wagtail foot

Thrush foot

Hind toe for grasping

FEET FOR PERCHING
Perching birds - a group that includes over half the world's species - all have a single hind toe. This toe enables the birds to get a tight grip on branches (opposite).

ALL-PURPOSE FEET
Like thrushes and wagtails, crows are perching birds, although they are among the largest members of this group. Crows' feet are like scaled-up versions of the feet of smaller perching birds, and have a large hind toe.

Crow foot

Hooked claws

Front toes

Rear toes

Green woodpecker foot

Greater spotted woodpecker foot

CLAWS FOR CLIMBING
Woodpeckers' feet have two toes pointing forward, and two pointing backward. This arrangement, which is unusual but not unique in the bird world, helps to anchor them as they chisel into wood.

DIFFERENT USES
Birds of prey spread their toes wide to catch their prey. Birds like the crow keep their toes closer together.

Outspread owl foot

Narrow crow foot

Feathers covering upper leg

BIRDS OF PREY
The feet of birds of prey are equipped with long talons and are so adapted to grasping prey that the birds have difficulty walking. Most birds of prey have feathered "trousers" that extend down to just below the ankle joint.

Sparrow hawk

Hidden ankle joint

Sparrow hawk foot

Talons

CARRIED ALOFT
The eagle's legendary grip enables it to carry heavy weights below its body and away from its wings.

Saw-whet owl foot

Insulating feathers covering toes

Talons

Saw-whet owl

FEATHERED TALONS
The feathers that cover the legs and feet of most owls help to silence their approach as they swoop down on prey.

WADERS

The weight of wading birds like curlews, and plovers is spread over elongated toes to keep them from sinking into soft mud. Many species, such as avocets, have exceptionally long legs for walking in deep water.

Hind toe

Gallinule foot

Long, widely spread toes to prevent sinking into soft mud

LILY TROTTER
Jacanas can walk over floating vegetation on their immensely long and thin toes.

Scaly flange aids swimming and prevents sinking in mud

Coot foot

THE COOT'S FLANGED FEET
The coot is unusual in having double flanges (ridges) of scaly skin that extend from each of the bones in its toes. When the coot swims, the flanges open out as the foot moves backward and close as it moves forward. On land, the flanges keep the coot from sinking in mud. The shape of the coot's feet produces footprints that are easy to tell from those of other water birds.

Canada goose foot

Webbed toes for swimming

WEBBED FEET
Ducks, geese, swans, gulls, and many seabirds have webbed feet for efficient swimming. Petrels can almost "walk" on water by pattering with their webbed feet while flapping their wings. Waterfowl use their feet as brakes when landing.

Coot

BIRD LEGS
In humans, the muscles that make the leg move are arranged all the way down its length. In birds, nearly all the muscles are at the top of the leg; the leg itself is little more than a bone surrounded by a pulley-like system of tendons all wrapped in scaly skin. This explains why some birds have such unbelievably thin legs: all the power that the leg needs is tucked away near the body.

Perching birds have evolved a special mechanism that keeps them from falling off perches. When a perching bird lands on a branch, its weight makes its leg tendons tighten and clamp its toes tightly shut. The bird has to make an effort not to stay on its perch, but to move off it. To take off, the bird contracts its toe muscles, the foot springs open, and it can then fly away.

Many birds that live in cold climates conserve their body heat by not wasting it on their legs. A network of blood vessels acts as a heat exchanger, taking heat out of blood destined to flow around the legs. Thus, the legs of birds such as gulls may be just a few degrees warmer than their icy surroundings.

Nuthatch landing

The structure of a bird's leg

Thigh bone

Knee joint

Ankle joint

Lower leg bone

Toes clamp to perch when bird rests its weight on the foot

Bird tracks

Birds move on the ground in one of two ways. Hopping is most common in smaller birds, which are able to lift their body weight easily by flexing the feet. Larger birds cannot hop and instead walk.

TRACKS IN MUD
Wet mud and fresh snow are the best surfaces for showing up bird tracks.

WALKING TRACKS
Hopping is not the best way for large birds to move around. Instead, they transfer their weight from foot to foot by walking.

Goose tracks

Finch tracks

HOPPING TRACKS
Small birds, especially woodland dwellers, hop on the ground.

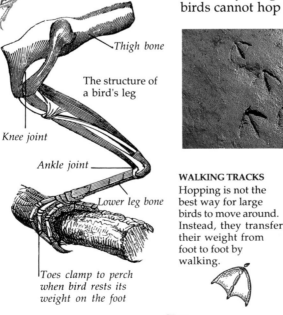

The senses

BIRDS LIVE IN A WORLD that is dominated by sight and sound. Their sense of vision is so highly developed that for most birds, three of the other four senses - touch, smell, and taste - are largely irrelevant. A hovering kestrel sees very much greater detail on the ground below it than a human would at the same height, but at the same time, scientists are not sure if birds can taste their prey. Humans have thousands of taste buds on their tongues, most birds have fewer than a hundred. However, birds have good hearing. They can distinguish notes that are far too fast for humans to separate. One species, the oilbird of South America, can use sound to navigate just like a bat. But with skulls packed with such sensitive eyes and ears, birds have not evolved large brains.

Members of the crow family, such as the raven, are the acknowledged intellectuals of the bird world

Raven skull

Separate bones in the cranium are fused together into a light-weight, but strong, protective case

Cranium

Nostril cavity connects with small paired nostrils that lie just behind the horny sheath of the beak

Opening to internal ear, usually hidden by a thin layer of short feathers

Eye socket points sideways in nearly all birds except those that catch fast-moving prey such as mammals and fish

Jugal (cheek) bone at base of eye socket supports a bird's large eyes

SENSES AND THE SKULL
Like all parts of the raven's body, its skull is modified to make it light enough for flying. In most animals, the separate bony plates that make up the cranium meet at long joints called sutures. In a bird's cranium, the separate bones are fused together for extra strength, allowing the bones themselves to be thinner. The eyes are often bigger than the brain. They are kept in their sockets by a ring of tiny bones attached to the bird's eyeball.

INTELLIGENCE AND INSTINCT
Birds' brains are small compared to those of mammals, and most birds are poor at learning new skills. However, a bird is born with a huge number of "programs" built into its brain. These programs control not only simple activities like preening and feeding, but also feats of instinct such as migration.

Optic lobe

Cerebellum

Cerebral hemisphere

Cerebellum

Optic lobe

Cerebral hemisphere

Spinal cord

The human's huge cerebral hemisphere allows rapid learning

Spinal cord

Much of the bird's brain is concerned with visual information

Cranium

Opposed eyes for wide-angle vision

Snipe skull

Bird vision

The eyes of owls point almost directly forward, giving them a wide field of binocular vision. This arrangement enables owls to judge distance very accurately, and it is shared by nearly all hunting birds. Birds that are themselves hunted tend to have eyes that point in opposite directions. The woodcock, for example, can see all around and above itself without moving its head. Most other birds' vision lies between these two extremes.

Monocular vision (left eye only)

Left eye

Owl

Right eye

Monocular vision (right eye only)

Binocular vision

REAR VIEW
Birds cannot swivel their eyeballs nearly as far as most other animals. An owl's eye movement, for example, is under two degrees, compared with 100 degrees for a human. Birds make up for this by having very flexible necks that can be turned to point backward.

Woodcock

Left eye

Monocular vision (left eye only)

Forward binocular vision

Blind spot

Rear binocular vision field enables bird to see enemies approaching from behind

Right eye

Monocular vision (right eye only)

Higher ear cavity

Lower ear cavity

The odd arrangement of an owl's ears is usually masked by its feathers

THE OWL'S UNBALANCED EARS
Owls hunt by night, when levels of light and sound are low. For this reason, an owl needs not only very acute vision but also extremely good hearing. Owls do not have external ears (although some species have earlike tufts of feathers). Instead their broad faces gather sound waves in the same way as an external ear and direct them to the eardrum within the skull. Owls' left and right ears are often at different levels in the skull. Each ear catches a sound at a slightly different time, giving improved "binaural" hearing which the owl uses to pinpoint its prey.

HUNTING IN DARKNESS
Some owls are able to hunt in complete darkness, using their ears to locate the sounds made by a scurrying animal.

Cranium

Hooked beak

Forward-pointing eye socket for binocular vision

Ear

Owl skull

SENSITIVE BEAKS
Like other animals, birds feel with sensitive receptors that are attached to nerves. These receptors are scattered all over the body, but in long-billed birds they are also found on the tip of the beak. When a wading bird probes into deep mud with its beak, it can actually feel what is below it.

Snipe

Elongated upper and lower jawbones of beak enable the snipe to reach food buried in mud

Sensitive tip of beak detects buried animals

FEELING FOR FOOD
Nightjars have bristles that extend forward from each side of their mouths. These are extremely fine, barbless feathers, probably used to funnel flying insects into the bird's mouth. Although birds do not have sensory hairs such as whiskers, it is possible that the nightjar can use its bristles to feel food.

Beaks

BECAUSE THEIR FRONT LIMBS are completely adapted for flight, most birds - with the important exception of parrots and birds of prey - catch and hold their food with their beaks alone. Birds' beaks have evolved a great variety of specialized shapes to enable them to tackle different kinds of food. This specialization was shown until recently by the huia of New Zealand. In this remarkable species, sadly now extinct, the male's beak was short and straight for probing, and the female's was long and curved for picking out insects.

Cone-shaped beak — Chaffinch

THE SEED CRACKER
A bird's beak produces the greatest force nearest its base. Birds like chaffinches, which live on hard seeds, have short, cone-shaped beaks so that they can crack open their food with as much force as possible. Finches deftly remove the cases of seeds with their beaks before swallowing them.

Sensitive tip for detecting worms in ground

Long beak for unearthing insect larvae and earthworms

A WADER ON DRY LAND
The woodcock's extremely long beak is typical of waders - the group of birds that includes plovers and sandpipers. But instead of using its beak to feed on shore animals, like most waders, the woodcock uses it equally as well on "dry" land. Its principal food is earthworms and insect larvae, and its long, pointed beak enables the woodcock to pluck these from damp ground.

Woodcock

Curlew

THE CURLEW'S FORCEPS
The curlew jabs its long beak into soft mud to pull out worms and mollusks that are beyond the reach of other birds.

Long, curled beak for digging up creatures buried deep in mud

In living bird, upper bill has a fringe to trap food

Lower bill pumps water against upper bill

Flamingo

Hinge of lower bill and skull

AN UNDERWATER SIEVE
The flamingo has one of the most specialized beaks of any bird. With its head pointing downward, the flamingo feeds by dipping its beak in water and using it to sift out nutritious water animals and plants. The lower bill moves up and down to pump water against the top bill, where a fringe of fine slits traps the food.

A MEAT-EATER'S BEAK
The kestrel has a hooked beak typical of falcons and other birds of prey. The hook enables these meat-eating birds to pull apart animals that are too big to be swallowed whole.

Hook

Kestrel

European blackbird

Medium-length pointed beak for seeds and larger food

A TWEEZER BEAK
The European blackbird has a beak shape that is shared by thousands of species of medium-size birds. It is sharply pointed to allow the bird to pick up small objects like seeds, but its length allows the bird to grasp larger food items such as earthworms. The male blackbird's orange-yellow beak is also used as a signal to female birds.

Parrot

Nostril

Area where seeds are cracked open

Hook for grasping fruit

A FRUIT-EATER'S BEAK
Wild parrots live on fruit and seeds and have a "combination" beak to allow them to make the most of their food. A parrot uses the hook at the beak's tip to pull at the pulp of fruit; it uses the jaws near the base of its beak to crack open seeds and reach the kernels. Parrots are unusual in the bird world in the way they also use their feet to hold and turn their food while they crack it open.

Teeth for catching fish, made out of the horny material of the beak

A BEAK FOR DABBLING
Many ducks feed by "dabbling," or opening and shutting the beak while skimming it across the water's surface. Water enters the two flattened halves of the beak, and anything in the water is strained out and swallowed. A duck's dabbling is rather like the sifting action of a flamingo, but a duck's beak is much less specialized and can be used for other kinds of feeding.

A DUCK WITH "TEETH"
Unlike mammals and reptiles, birds do not have true teeth that are made of bone. However, some birds have evolved structures that are very like teeth. The mergansers, for example, have tooth-like notches on the sides of their beaks. They use these beak teeth to catch fish, both in fresh water and out at sea.

Merganser

Flattened beak

Long, hooked beak for catching fish and ripping them apart

ALL-PURPOSE BEAK
Gulls' beaks are long and end in a hook that is smaller but in many ways similar to that of meat-eating birds. This beak shape not only enables a gull to catch and hold prey like fish along the length of the beak, but also allows them to pull apart their food.

Gull

Scoter

Plant and insect eaters

THE WORLD'S MOST NUMEROUS wild bird, the red-billed quelea, is a seed eater. Over one hundred billion of these birds scour African fields and grassland for food, forming flocks that are millions strong. Birds like the quelea can survive in huge numbers because they live on a food that is incredibly abundant. Seeds, grass, nectar, insects, worms, and many other small animals exist in vast amounts, and together they form the food for the majority of the world's birds.

Thrush

Eating plants and seeds

Birds that eat plants and seeds have to crush their food before they can digest it. As they have no teeth, they do this with powerful beaks and also with the gizzard (p. 8) - a muscular "grinding chamber" in their stomachs.

Finch skull

Hard-cased seeds

Goose skull

SPECIALIST SEED EATERS
Finches, which number over 150 species, have short, sharp bills for breaking open seeds and nuts. Amazingly, some finches have bills that can exert more crushing force than a human hand.

Leaf crops

Pigeon skull

FEEDING ON CROPS
Pigeons and doves originally ate the leaves and seeds of wild plants; now they often feed on cultivated ones as well. They can also use their pointed bills like a straw when drinking - a unique ability among birds.

Cultivated grain

LIVING ON GRASS
Geese are among the few kinds of birds that can live on a diet of grass. But geese digest grass poorly, and it passes through their bodies in just two hours. Because they get so little out of their food, they must eat a lot of it and so feed almost constantly.

Broad bill for tearing grass

Capercaillie skull

Powerful hooked beak for grasping leaves from trees and crushing seeds

ALL-AROUND PLANT EATERS
Game birds - species like pheasants, grouse, and this capercaillie from northern Europe - eat whatever plant food is available, although their preference is for seeds. In winter, the capercaillie lives on the leaves of cone-bearing trees, a source of food that few other animals use. It pulls the leaves from branches with its powerful hooked beak

Seeds

Needles of cone-bearing trees

The grass and water plants on which geese feed

Invertebrate eaters

Every spring, the number of insects and other invertebrates (animals without backbones) increases dramatically. These animals form the food for dozens of species of migratory birds. In winter, the supply is much smaller and food is harder to find, consisting mainly of larvae (grubs) in wood or in the soil. These are sought out by specialist insect eaters.

Blackcap skull

Aphids

Caterpillar

PROBING WARBLERS
These small songsters use their delicate probing beaks to pick insects from leaves and bark. When the supply dries up in early autumn, they migrate south.

THE SNAIL SMASHER
Thrushes eat a wide range of food, both plant and animal. Some feed on snails, which they smash open on stone "anvils."

Thrush skull

Snail shells broken open by thrush

Woodpecker skull

Centipede

Beetle larvae

Adult beetle

Earthworms are eaten not only by garden birds, but also by some owls and even birds of prey

Pecked apple

LARGE INSECT EATERS
Birds like woodpeckers and the mainly ground-feeding hoopoe use their beaks to pick large insects out of crevices in trees. Woodpeckers also chisel into the wood to find concealed grubs. Their extremely long tongues have spearlike tips that are used for stabbing their prey.

Hoopoe skull

Avocet feeding

Feeding on the shore

Although there are very few salt-water insects, the seashore contains a year-round supply of other invertebrates for birds to eat, from crabs and shellfish to burrowing worms.

Ribbon worm

Silt-burrowing lugworm

Avocet skull

THE SWEEP-NET BEAK
The avocet catches worms and other prey by striding forward and sweeping its beak from side to side. It is one of the very few birds with an upturned beak.

Worms

Crab broken open and eaten; the hard skeleton is usually discarded

Oyster catcher skull

Mussel

A BUILT-IN HAMMER
The oyster catcher feeds on seashore animals with hard shells. It has a long beak like the avocet, but instead of ending in a fine point, its tip is blunt. This built-in "hammer" enables the oyster catcher to smash through the shells of its prey. Such feeding needs a great deal of skill, and some oyster catchers prize shells open instead. An experienced bird will know precisely where the weak points are on a mussel or cockleshell, and if the shell is lying on sand, the bird will carry it to a rock to break it open.

Cockles

Hunters, fishers, and all-arounders

FLIGHT ENABLES BIRDS to cover great distances in search of food. This gives them a big advantage as predators, because few animals - on land or far out at sea - are beyond their reach. Flight also makes birds very effective all-around feeders. A dead animal, an unprotected nest, or a field of ripening crops is quickly spotted by passing birds and turned into a satisfying meal.

Kingfishers

Meat and fish eaters

Birds that feed on larger animals and fish catch their prey in two different ways. Most fish eaters use their beaks to catch their quarry. On land, birds of prey use their talons for catching and their beaks for tearing.

Strips of meat torn from prey with powerful hooked beak

Tawny owl skull

Fur is swallowed and later discarded in pellets

Buzzard skull

NIGHT AND DAY HUNTERS
In general, owls and birds of prey such as the buzzard operate like two sets of shift workers, catching rodents and larger mammals around the clock. A few owls do hunt by day, but no bird of prey can hunt during the night because their eyesight and hearing is not good enough.

Large forward-pointing eyes enable the gannet to pinpoint fish below

Halves of the beak meet at a long straight line for holding fish before they are swallowed

Streamlined point for diving

Gannet skull

ABOVE AND BELOW WATER
Gannets dive-bomb shoals of fish by plunging, with their wings folded, from heights of up to 100 ft (30 m). They stay below the surface for only a few seconds. Cormorants pursue fish underwater. Their feathers do not trap air like those of other water birds, and this enables them to dive swiftly and overtake their prey.

PATIENCE REWARDED
The heron fishes by stealth, staying motionless until its prey swims within reach of its long stabbing beak.

Hooked beak for grasping fish

Cormorant skull

Mackerel

A mixed diet

It doesn't take much intelligence to be a successful seed eater, but birds that survive on a mixed diet must live by their wits. These scavengers are quick to take a chance that might lead to a meal; other birds would hesitate and miss out. They thrive on waste food and household rubbish, as well as more natural food items.

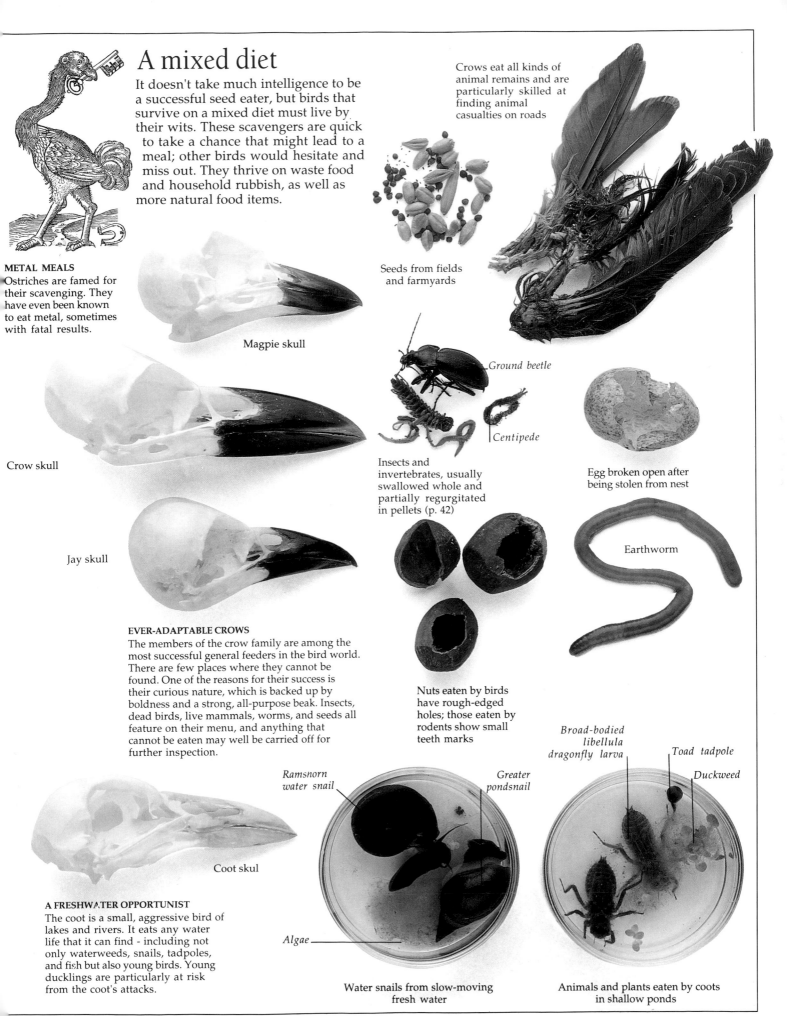

METAL MEALS
Ostriches are famed for their scavenging. They have even been known to eat metal, sometimes with fatal results.

Magpie skull

Crow skull

Jay skull

EVER-ADAPTABLE CROWS
The members of the crow family are among the most successful general feeders in the bird world. There are few places where they cannot be found. One of the reasons for their success is their curious nature, which is backed up by boldness and a strong, all-purpose beak. Insects, dead birds, live mammals, worms, and seeds all feature on their menu, and anything that cannot be eaten may well be carried off for further inspection.

Coot skul

A FRESHWATER OPPORTUNIST
The coot is a small, aggressive bird of lakes and rivers. It eats any water life that it can find - including not only waterweeds, snails, tadpoles, and fish but also young birds. Young ducklings are particularly at risk from the coot's attacks.

Crows eat all kinds of animal remains and are particularly skilled at finding animal casualties on roads

Seeds from fields and farmyards

Ground beetle

Centipede

Insects and invertebrates, usually swallowed whole and partially regurgitated in pellets (p. 42)

Egg broken open after being stolen from nest

Earthworm

Nuts eaten by birds have rough-edged holes; those eaten by rodents show small teeth marks

Ramsnorn water snail

Greater pondsnail

Broad-bodied libellula dragonfly larva

Toad tadpole

Duckweed

Algae

Water snails from slow-moving fresh water

Animals and plants eaten by coots in shallow ponds

Pellets

PREDATORY BIRDS like owls feed on small mammals and birds, but because they do not have teeth, they cannot chew their food. Instead, they either rip their prey apart with their claws or eat it whole. This means that they swallow large quantities of bones, fur, and feathers, which they cannot digest. So once or twice a day they regurgitate (expel through the mouth) these items, packed tightly together, as pellets. The shape of a pellet identifies the species of bird that produced it, and the contents of the pellet show what the bird has been eating.

PELLETS IN OPEN GROUND
The short-eared owl hunts in daylight over rough grassland and marshes, catching voles and sometimes young birds. Its pellets are long, with rounded ends. This particular species of owl does not drop its pellets from a perch but scatters them around low clumps of grass.

Rounded ends

Limb bone from a rodent

Smooth dark crust

Blunt ends

PELLETS BENEATH A ROOST
The smooth, almost black pellets of the barn owl are easy to identify. They often accumulate in small piles beneath roosts in old barns and other buildings.

Recent pellet still in compact state

Older pellet beginning to disintegrate

Pointed ends

Protruding bones, typical of tawny owl pellets

Beetle wing case

Earth and fur

PELLETS IN PARKS AND GARDENS
Tawny owl pellets are the only ones commonly found in parks - where the owl often nests - in suburbs, and also in the countryside. Tawny owls eat voles, mice, shrews, and birds, as well as much smaller animals. Their pellets are smooth and sometimes have pointed ends. Pellets that have been on the ground for a while often crumble to reveal a mass of protruding bones and tangled fur.

A VARIED DIET
All these pellets are from little owls. They show how a bird's diet can change the appearance of its pellets. The smaller pellets contain fur and earth - the earth having been produced by a meal of earthworms. The larger pellets also contain earth and small amounts of fur, but packed into this are the legs and wing cases of beetles.

Beetle leg

Shell fragments

Wing cases of beetles mixed in with plant material

Seeds left behind after the soft flesh of berries has been digested

Rodent limb bone

Seed cases mixed with pieces of shell

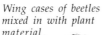

Tin foil

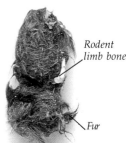

Fur

WADER PELLETS
The curlew and many other wading birds eat hard-shelled animals such as crabs. Their pellets contain pieces of these shells, sometimes mixed with the cases of seeds.

CROW PELLETS
Crows and their relatives eat all kinds of food. Their pellets often contain insect remains and plant stalks.

SONGBIRD PELLETS
Thrushes and blackbirds produce pellets that contain seeds. This specimen also contains a small piece of tin foil.

FALCON PELLETS
Birds like the kestrel and peregrine falcon produce pellets that contain bird, mammal, and insect remains.

Inside an owl pellet

By pulling apart a pellet, it is possible to find out something about an owl's diet. Here two tawny owl pellets have been carefully taken apart. The first pellet shows that the owl that produced it had dined entirely on voles - three of these small mammals made up the bird's nightly catch. The second pellet tells a rather different and more surprising story.

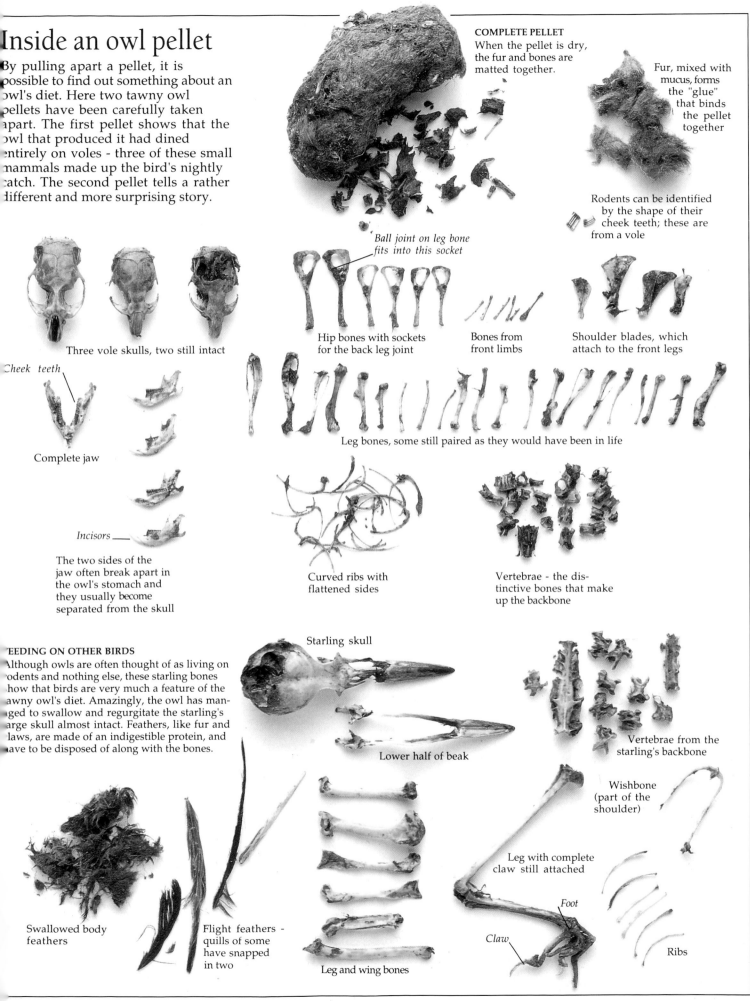

COMPLETE PELLET
When the pellet is dry, the fur and bones are matted together.

Fur, mixed with mucus, forms the "glue" that binds the pellet together

Rodents can be identified by the shape of their cheek teeth; these are from a vole

Ball joint on leg bone fits into this socket

Hip bones with sockets for the back leg joint

Bones from front limbs

Shoulder blades, which attach to the front legs

Leg bones, some still paired as they would have been in life

Three vole skulls, two still intact

Cheek teeth

Complete jaw

Incisors

The two sides of the jaw often break apart in the owl's stomach and they usually become separated from the skull

Curved ribs with flattened sides

Vertebrae - the distinctive bones that make up the backbone

FEEDING ON OTHER BIRDS

Although owls are often thought of as living on rodents and nothing else, these starling bones show that birds are very much a feature of the tawny owl's diet. Amazingly, the owl has managed to swallow and regurgitate the starling's large skull almost intact. Feathers, like fur and claws, are made of an indigestible protein, and have to be disposed of along with the bones.

Starling skull

Lower half of beak

Vertebrae from the starling's backbone

Wishbone (part of the shoulder)

Leg with complete claw still attached

Foot

Claw

Ribs

Swallowed body feathers

Flight feathers - quills of some have snapped in two

Leg and wing bones

43

Making a nest

NEST BUILDING is a job with two parts that are done at the same time: collecting the materials and fashioning them into the finished nest. The amount of time spent collecting depends on how far away the materials are: a reed warbler hardly has to move to find dry reed leaves, but a swallow must find a puddle that will provide exactly the kind of mud it needs. Birds go through a special series of movements to work materials into their nests. When a cup nester returns to the nest with materials, it first pushes them roughly into place. The bird then sits in the center of the nest and begins to turn around and around, pushing downward and outward with its breast. This circular movement, which gives the inside of the nest its shape, is shared by all birds. Cup nesters turn and push; birds such as herons turn and trample, pulling at individual sticks on the nest platform as they do so.

NATURAL MATERIALS

Nest materials have two main functions: support and insulation. Most hedgerow and woodland birds use sticks for the main structure of their nests, then add an insulating lining which may be of feathers, seed heads, or animal fur. House martins and some swallows make their nests entirely out of mud. Another insect eater, the swift, collects nesting material in midair by catching floating fibers in its beak.

MUD
Mixed with saliva to form a sticky paste.

SEED HEADS
Used in the nest lining for insulation.

LEAVES AND NEEDLES
Used for the inside of many cup nests.

TWIGS AND STICKS
Main structural material in larger nests.

MAN-MADE MATERIALS

Anything that can be carried away may end up in a bird's nest. Pigeons have been found nesting, quite literally, on beds of nails, and coots on plastic bags. Storks may use old clothes and other rubbish to build their massive nests.

Hooded crow

STRING
Small lengths are found in many nests.

TIN FOIL
Often collected by crows and magpies.

PLASTIC BALER TWINE
A favorite with birds nesting on farmland.

PAPER AND TISSUE
Found in the nests of many city birds.

Nest ingredients

Packed with a huge variety of ingredients, the pied wagtail's nest shown here is like a guide to a complete habitat. Its owner has scoured fields, hedgerows, old walls, and fences for plant and animal materials, making hundreds or perhaps thousands of trips to bring all that it has collected back to the growing nest.

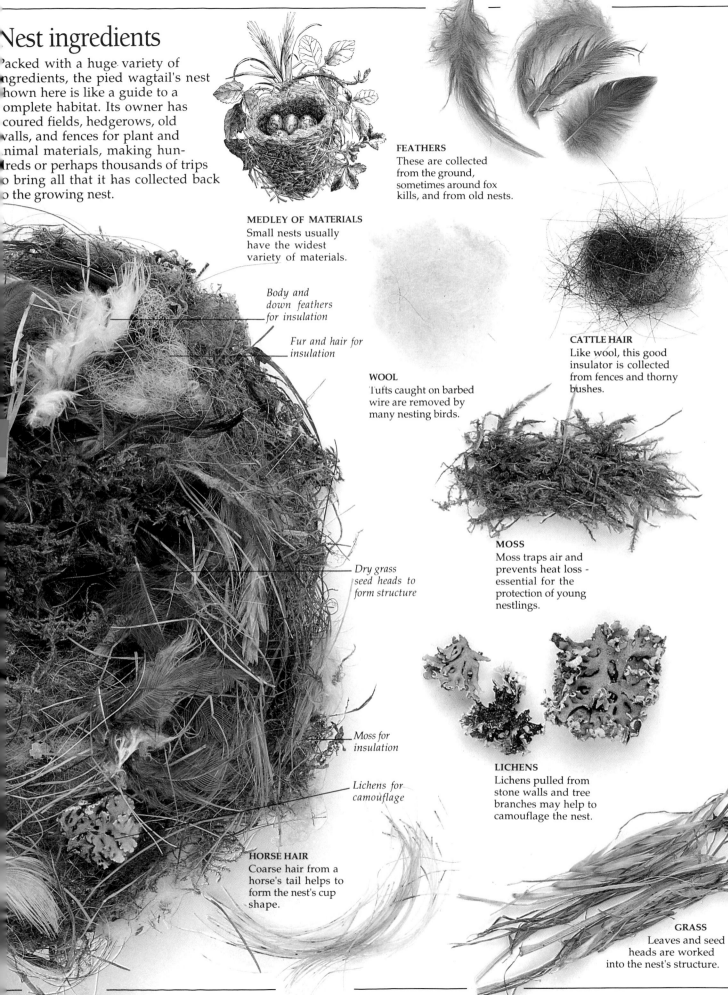

FEATHERS
These are collected from the ground, sometimes around fox kills, and from old nests.

MEDLEY OF MATERIALS
Small nests usually have the widest variety of materials.

Body and down feathers for insulation

Fur and hair for insulation

WOOL
Tufts caught on barbed wire are removed by many nesting birds.

CATTLE HAIR
Like wool, this good insulator is collected from fences and thorny bushes.

Dry grass seed heads to form structure

MOSS
Moss traps air and prevents heat loss - essential for the protection of young nestlings.

Moss for insulation

Lichens for camouflage

LICHENS
Lichens pulled from stone walls and tree branches may help to camouflage the nest.

HORSE HAIR
Coarse hair from a horse's tail helps to form the nest's cup shape.

GRASS
Leaves and seed heads are worked into the nest's structure.

Cup nests

BIRD NESTS COME IN ALL SHAPES AND SIZES. They can be tiny shelves of saliva that are glued to the walls of caves, long tunnels that run many yards into the ground, or, in the case of some eagles, massive piles of branches that weigh more than a family-size car. But the most familiar nests are undoubtedly the cup nests, which are built by birds of woodland, hedgerows, and farmland. Despite their overall similarity, the fine details of these nests identify their makers as surely as a fingerprint.

Chaffinch at nest

Rooks nesting on a weathervane

Moss and lichen cup forms the main structure of the nest

Feathers from other birds provide insulation

Dried moss

Hair and feather lining insulates the eggs and developing nestlings

Redstart

SPIDERWEB FOUNDATIONS

To make its nest, a chaffinch first loops strands of spiders' webs around a group of forked branches. These are the anchors for the nest; once they are secure, the bird builds up the cup with moss, lichens, and grass, then lines it with feathers and hair. Collecting these nesting materials takes a long time. If for any reason the chaffinch decides that its nest site is unsafe, it will transfer materials from the old nest to a new site to avoid too much extra work.

SECONDHAND FEATHERED LINING

Feathers are an important part of many birds' nests. Songbirds like the redstart, whose nest is shown here, collect feathers shed by other birds. Water fowl and waders use their own feathers. Some small birds, such as sparrows, improve on the natural supply by pulling feathers from the backs of larger birds.

Mud lining

Song thrush feeding young

MASTERPIECE IN MUD

Many cup-nest builders use mud to make their nests, in most cases applying it as a layer just beneath a final lining of feathers, hair, or grass. The song thrush is unusual in choosing mud as the lining itself. The bird makes a strong outer cup of twigs and grass, and then it smears the semi-liquid lining around the inside. Although mud makes up most of the mixture, it also contains saliva and animal droppings. Once the lining has been applied, it becomes hard. Even after the birds have left the nest it can withstand rain for many months.

Outer cup

Nests on buildings

Although it has taken birds millions of years to develop their nest-building skills, they are surprisingly quick to make use of any new sites that become available. Stone and brick houses are a relatively recent feature on the Earth. However, in the few thousand years that buildings have been around, some birds, especially house martins, swifts, swallows, and storks, have taken up residence on them in large numbers. Walls and window ledges make an ideal home for cliffs-nesting birds; rooftops and chimneys are used by birds that originally nested in treetops; and kettles, shelves and tool sheds are used by hedgerow species.

TREE SUBSTITUTE
Storks pile up their stick nests on chimneys and the tops of buildings. A pair of storks returns to the same site year after year.

ARTIFICIAL CLIFFS
Swallows and martins glue their mud nests onto ledges and vertical walls.

HEDGEROW HEIGHT
Hedge birds pick sites by height. This broom is right for a blackbird.

Nightingale with young

READY FOR RECYCLING
Some cup nests are carefully shaped and lined; others are less skillfully built. This nightingale's nest is made of reeds and grass. Loose nests like this may be taken apart by other birds for "recycling" after their owners have left them.

Reeds

Loosely made structure of leaves, grass and reeds

Grass lining on inside of cup

Lining made entirely of hair collected from ferns and bark against which animals have rubbed

Outer cup made of grass, leaves and stems matted together

A HAIR-FILLED NEST
Reed buntings build their small cup-shaped nests on or near the ground. The building bird (in this case, always the female) starts by making a frame of thick grass. Once this is finished, she adds the lining - a deep layer of fur or hair. This she plucks either from the thorns of hedgerow shrubs or from the barbs of barbed wire.

Female reed bunting at nest

Unusual nests

THE ANCESTORS of modern birds probably made nests that were simply hollows in the ground. Although some birds still do nest like this, others have raised nest building to a supreme craft, weaving nests of astounding complexity. But amazingly, none of these bird architects has any real understanding of what they are doing. Nest building is entirely instinctive; although a bird gets better with practice, it needs no training and is unable to depart from its blueprint.

Nest chamber

Twig forming a support for the nest

String

Cattle hair

STRING NEST
The Baltimore oriole is a familiar summer visitor to farmlands. Like all birds that nest near people, it has an eye for man-made materials that might be useful in building its baglike nest. This particular nest is made up of cattle hair and a large amount of string. The bird has skillfully wound some string around a twig to form a support.

Baltimore oriole perching above its distinctive bag-like nest

HOME SECURITY
This extraordinary trumpet-shaped nest was built by a West African weaver bird. Weavers are special in being able to tie knots with their beaks and feet. The long trumpet of this bird's nest keeps predatory snakes from getting inside.

1

2

3

WEAVER AT WORK
Weaver nests begin as a knotted ring that is then extended downward to form a round chamber. An entrance funnel may then be added.

Grasses weaved together to form a tube

Entrance funnel to guard against snakes

SPLIT DUTIES

The male village weaver does nearly all the outside work in making this complicated bell-shaped nest. When the structure is complete, he flutters around the nest to entice a mate to inspect it. Once a female has approved his work and moved in, she completes the interior lining. By the time she is sitting on her clutch of eggs, the male will have started on a new nest. However, it is unlikely that he will move far away: like most weavers, the village weaver is a highly social bird - hundreds of individuals may build their nests in the same tree.

Thorn tree twig

Nest made of reed flowers, grass, and feathers

Reed warbler with nestlings

Nest chamber

Entrance

Grass strands

Reeds

MULTISTOREY NEST
In reality, weavers' nests do not share the same entrance as suggested by this fanciful engraving.

Feathers

Interlocking mixture of moss, hair, and spider webs

Entrance hole

A REEDBED BASKET
The reed warbler's nest is slung between dried stems deep in a reedbed. Building the cup-shaped nest calls for some acrobatic skill, especially since the different stems to which the nest is attached often blow about in the wind. The nest is held in place with "handles" similar to those on a basket, and both male and female birds build on these foundations by adding reed flowers, grass, and feathers.

Nest of penduline tit

CRAMPED QUARTERS
Although only about 7 in (18 cm) from top to bottom, the long-tailed tit's nest is one of the most elaborate outside the tropics. It is made up of spider webs, moss, and hair and is lined with hundreds of tiny feathers. However, it is so cramped that the female can fit inside only by curling her tail against the nest.

SHARED HOUSING
Some birds live together in large groups, but their nests are never quite this elegant.

Eggs of water birds and waders

THE KIND OF EGG that a bird lays depends on how it lives. True seabirds (ones that come ashore only to breed) usually lay a single egg on rocky ledges away from enemies. Wading birds lay more eggs, but on the coasts and inlets there is little cover for their nests, so their eggs are camouflaged.

Gulls

WARNING All the eggs shown here come from established museum collections. Collecting or handling wild birds' eggs is now illegal.

FOSTERED EGGS
A gallinule may sneak the first of its clutch of eggs into another bird's nest for the unsuspecting neighbor to look after. After this, the gallinule settles down to raise up to a dozen of its own eggs itself.

Shoveler duck

Undersize egg

Normal egg

A TERN'S EGGS
Least terns lay two or three eggs at a time in a hollow in the ground, usually in a pile of pebbles. The eggs' delicate patterning makes them almost impossible to see against the surrounding pebbles.

VARIATIONS IN SIZE
Just as a litter of mammals may contain an undersize specimen, so occasionally may a clutch of eggs. These two eggs are both from a shoveler duck. Like most ducks, it produces a large number of eggs - between eight and 12 in a nest.

EGGS UNDER GUARD
Common tern eggs are fearlessly defended by their parents. During incubation, the birds attack any intruder - even humans - by diving directly at them.

GULL EGGS
Many gulls lay their eggs on the ground, where camouflage is important. This egg is from one of the largest gulls, the great black-backed gull. Its speckled color hides it from predators, which can include other gulls, during the four weeks it takes to hatch.

THE EGG THAT ROLLS BACK
The murre produces one of the most unusually shaped and differently colored eggs of all birds. Murres do not build nests. Instead, each female lays its single egg directly on a bare cliff ledge. The egg's pointed shape helps to keep her from accidentally knocking it off its risky spot. Should it begin to roll, it will travel back in a circle rather than on in a straight line. The different colors are more difficult to explain. They may help parents to recognize their own egg among the thousands in a murre colony.

Murre

Cream and brown form

White form

Streaked gray form

50

CAMOUFLAGE AND CONFUSION
The little ringed plover lays its eggs on gravel and pebbles near water, where the eggs are protected by their camouflage coloring. If an intruder approaches the nest, the parent birds often fly directly at it, toward the source of danger, veering away at the last minute in an attempt to distract attention from the eggs. When the eggs have hatched, this distraction display becomes even more complicated, with the parents scuttling away from the nestlings to confuse enemies.

SLOW DEVELOPER
The fulmar's single egg needs a long seven and a half weeks of incubation before it will hatch. The egg is laid on a cliff ledge. Its color shows that there is little need for camouflage so far beyond the reach of land predators.

Egg from speckled clutch

Egg from dark clutch

Egg from light clutch

COLORS IN A CLUTCH
Each of these three eggs comes from a small wading bird. Many camouflaged eggs vary widely in both pattern and color between clutches. However, within a single clutch the eggs are much more closely matched.

Woodcock

THE DOUBLE-POINTED EGG
The great crested grebe lays its curiously shaped eggs on a mound of waterlogged vegetation. Most grebes have unusually pointed eggs, but no one knows why.

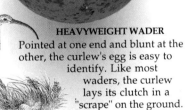

Curlew

HEAVYWEIGHT WADER
Pointed at one end and blunt at the other, the curlew's egg is easy to identify. Like most waders, the curlew lays its clutch in a "scrape" on the ground.

CONCEALED IN THE TREETOPS
The gray heron builds its nest high in the trees, so its blue eggs are rarely seen in one piece. When fresh, this egg was bright blue, but the color has faded over the years.

AT THE WATER'S EDGE
Loons are freshwater fish-eating birds. They are clumsy on land, so they lay their dark brown eggs right by the water's edge to reduce the risk of damage.

RECORD INCUBATION
The albatross lays the largest and heaviest egg of any seabird, with some specimens weighing more than 1.1 lb (500 g). Albatross eggs have the longest incubation period of any bird: parents sit on a single egg for two and a half months.

Albatross

Eggs of land birds

SMALL LAND BIRDS, like the seed and insect eaters, lay small eggs. However, many produce large clutches - sometimes well over a dozen eggs. Others get through their breeding cycle very quickly and cram a number of clutches into a single season. Large birds, on the other hand, lay far fewer eggs. For birds such as eagles and vultures, one small clutch a year is all they produce.

Some of the specimens shown have lost the brightness of their original colors due to age

HIDDEN IN THE UNDERGROWTH
The nightingale makes its nest in low, tangled bushes. Its brown eggs are well hidden in the shadows cast by leaves and branches.

Coal tit egg

Blue tit egg

HEAVYWEIGHT CLUTCH
Tits, including the coal tit, blue tit, and American chickadee, lay up to 15 eggs, each clutch weighing up to a third more than the bird.

Wood warbler egg   Marsh warbler egg

SUMMER VISITORS
Most of the world's 400 species of warbler migrate to breed. They arrive at the same time as the annual insect population explosion, which provides food for the average family of six nestlings.

Chaffinch egg   Hawfinch egg

SLOW BEGINNERS
Finches lay betweeen four and six eggs in trees and bushes. Some finches do not lay eggs until early summer when seeds, their staple food, become available.

DOWN ON THE GROUND
Buntings are sparrow-like birds that lay their eggs on or near the ground. This is the egg of a corn bunting, a species unusual in that up to seven females may share the same mate.

Tawny owl egg

Little owl egg

Baltimore oriole

HIGHLY VISIBLE EGGS
Owl eggs are white, almost round, and have a glossy surface. The round shape is typical of many eggs laid in holes. They might be white so the parent bird can see them, or the color may have evolved because there is no need for camouflage.

Long-eared owl

ADDED COLOR
Surface colors like the brown and gray streaks on this Baltimore oriole's egg are formed just a few hours before the egg is laid.

LESS TO LAY
The wood pigeon, a typical medium-size bird, lays two eggs. Together they weigh less than a tenth of the parent - a tiny proportion compared to the eggs of smaller birds.

THE CHIMNEY NESTER
The jackdaw, a member of the crow family, lays its eggs in holes, either in trees, rocky outcrops, or buildings. Chimneys are one of its favorite nesting sites - sometimes with disastrous results.

Normal egg   Outsize egg

ABNORMAL EGGS
During the process of egg production, things sometimes go wrong. A single egg may have two yolks, or it may be of a different size to a normal egg. The eggs shown here are crow's eggs.

Carrion crow

MOORLAND CAMOUFLAGE
One look at a grouse's camouflaged egg shows that this bird nests on the ground. Dark blotches help to conceal clutches of up to ten eggs during the month-long incubation among heather and bracken.

Cuckoo egg

Cuckoo egg

European robin egg

THE CUCKOO'S DECEPTION
Cuckoos lay their eggs in the nests of other birds. The host birds, such as robins, are always much smaller than the cuckoo, but the cuckoo lays tiny eggs for a bird of its size. Here, a cuckoo has tried to match the color of its egg (above) with those laid by a European robin.

Cuckoo

Dunnock egg

Cuckoo egg

A POOR MATCH
The European cuckoo has too many hosts to match all their eggs.

AMERICAN ROBIN
This bird is a member of the thrush family, unlike the European robin.

NONSTOP PRODUCTION
The European blackbird's clutch of four eggs is typical of members of the thrush family. They all have the ability to raise more than one family in a year. If conditions are especially good, a female blackbird can lay up to five clutches in a season. However, winter takes its toll on many of the offspring, and few survive into the following year.

DAYTIME DISGUISE
The nocturnal nightjar does not make a nest. Instead, it lays its pair of eggs on rough ground. The eggs' camouflage is almost as good as the parent bird's (p. 30).

HOLE NESTER
Many woodpeckers chisel out nest holes in trees. Their eggs are very similar to those of hole-nesting owls - white and glossy.

RAISED AMONG THE ROOFTOPS
The kestrel lays a clutch of four to six eggs. It occasionally nests on city buildings, where its eggs perch at great risk on gutters and window ledges.

VULNERABLE HAWKS
Sparrowhawks once suffered as a result of poisoning caused by the insecticide DDT, though numbers have now recovered. Although bright blue when laid, the egg color fades.

FISH-EATING FALCON
The osprey - one of the most widely distributed birds in the world - has eggs of highly variable color. They take about five weeks to be incubated.

OLD WORLD VULTURE
The Egyptian vulture lays its eggs high up on cliffs and in cave mouths. As an adult, it feeds on the eggs of other large birds, smashing them open with a stone.

ONE OF A PAIR
Eagles lay eggs in clutches of two. Unlike small birds, which lay an egg a day, eagles leave an interval of several days between laying the first and second egg.

SLOW DEVELOPERS
Buzzards lay between two and four eggs in a clutch. Incubation takes over five weeks and the nestlings stay in the nest for another six weeks. As a result, parents can raise only one clutch a year.

Extraordinary eggs

THE LARGEST living bird, the ostrich, lays an egg that is 4,500 times heavier than that of the smallest, a hummingbird. But going back in time, one of the heaviest birds that ever existed - the elephant bird - laid eggs that could each have swallowed up seven ostrich eggs with room to spare. The extraordinary differences in sizes of bird species is demonstrated especially vividly by their eggs.

THE ROC
This creature from the *Arabian Nights* may have actually existed, not as an inhabitant of the air, but as the huge and flightless elephant bird of Madagascar.

HUMMINGBIRD EGG
Each egg weighs about one fifth of the adult's weight.

OSTRICH EGG
Each egg weighs up to 3.3 lb (1.5 kg) - about one hundredth of the adult's weight.

Hummingbirds

LIGHTER THAN FEATHERS
Hummingbirds lay the smallest eggs of any bird. The very tiniest of them measures about 0.4 in (1 cm) from end to end and weighs about 0.01 oz (0.35 g). Hummingbird eggs are long with rounded edges, and only two are laid in the tiny, cup-shaped nest. It takes about three weeks for the nestlings to grow all their feathers and leave the nest to fend for themselves.

Shell almost 2 mm thick

CLUBBING TOGETHER
The ostrich lays the largest egg of any bird alive today. Although a single hen lays a clutch of about 10, more than one bird may lay in the same place, helping to create an unmanageable pile of perhaps as many as 50 eggs.

Ostrich

EMU EGG
The egg weighs just over one hundredth of the adult's weight.

KIWI EGG
The egg is nearly one quarter of the adult's weight.

AN EGG THAT CHANGES COLOR
When they are laid, the eggs of the Australian emu are a dull green color, but within a few days they turn black and glossy. Like the ostrich, the emu lays a lot of eggs - up to 10 weighing 1.5 lb (700 g) each.

Emu

Kiwi

THE KIWI'S OUTSIZE EGG
The chicken-sized kiwi lays the largest egg in relation to her body of any bird. Each egg weighs about 1 lb (450 g) and normally the 3.75 lb (1.7 kg) female kiwi lays just one. Her labors are far from over once the egg has been laid: incubation lasts nearly two and a half months.

ELEPHANT BIRD EGG
The egg weighed about three percent of the adult's body weight.

THE LARGEST EGG
The bird that laid this monster egg - *Aepyornis titan*, or the elephant bird - weighed nearly half a ton, and its huge eggs tipped the scales at 26 lb (12 kg) each, making them the largest ever laid. Elephant birds lived in Madagascar, and although they died out about 700 years ago, whole eggs and shattered shells have been uncovered in the island's swamps. Elephant bird eggs easily outclass those of the dinosaurs - the volume of the bird's egg being over twice that of any dinosaur egg.

Hatching

F OR SOMETHING SO LIGHT, the shell of an egg is extremely strong, and a hatching bird must spend hours or even days of hard labor in breaking this barrier to the outside world. Some birds hatch in a poorly developed state. As nestlings, they are helpless and depend completely on their parents for food. However, "precocial" birds, such as the pheasant shown here, are well developed on hatching and can soon fend for themselves.

INSIDE THE EGG
Development of the embryo starts as soon as the mother begins incubation.

Albumen
Yolk
Embryo
Protein cord
1

Air sac
Sac for waste products
Embryo
2

Developing chick
Shrinking yolk sac
3

1 PREPARING FOR HATCHING
Hatching for a pheasant chick, like that of other birds, begins invisibly. The chick, still completely enclosed in the shell, turns around so that its beak is pointing toward the egg's blunt end. Then, with a sudden movement of its head, it pecks at the air sac. This is a crucial part of the chick's development because, by breaking into the sac, the chick is able to breathe air for the first time. Once its lungs are functioning, the chick may call to its mother from inside the egg. These calls probably help to prepare her for the onset of hatching.

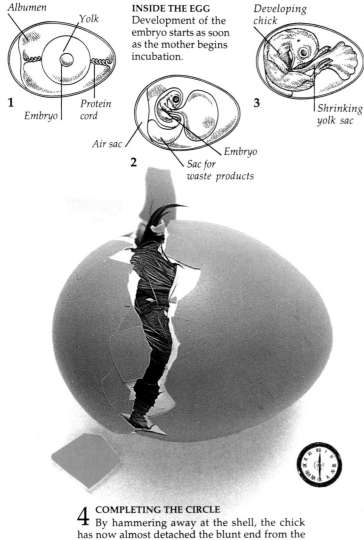

4 COMPLETING THE CIRCLE
By hammering away at the shell, the chick has now almost detached the blunt end from the rest of the egg. Large pieces of shell fall away from the egg as the chick struggles to finish its labors. An entire clutch of pheasant eggs hatches within a few hours, so by the time the chick has reached this stage, many of its brothers and sisters may have already hatched.

5 GETTING A GRIP
Having cut a complete circle through the shell, the chick begins to emerge from the egg. From now on, things happen very quickly. The chick first hooks its toes over the lip of the shell (the toes are just visible here), and then, having gotten a good grip, it starts to push with its feet and shoulders. With a few heaves, the egg's blunt end is lifted away.

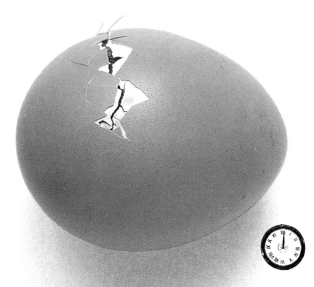

2 BREAKING THE SHELL

Hatching begins in earnest when, after several attempts, the chick finally breaks through the shell. It does this with the help of two special adaptations. The first is the "egg tooth," a small projection on its beak that breaks the shell and falls off soon after hatching. The second is a powerful muscle behind the head that powers the egg tooth's blows. Between pecking sessions, the chick stops for long rests.

3 CUTTING A CIRCLE

Having broken open the shell, the chick sets about extending the initial crack sideways. After each bout of pecking, it stops and turns itself slightly by pushing with its feet. The chick's repeated pecking and turning produces a crack that runs neatly around the base of the egg's blunt end. This will eventually allow the blunt end to be pushed away.

Egg tooth

6 BREAKING OUT

With its feet clearly visible, the chick gives another push and the blunt end of the egg comes away, sitting like a hat on the chick's head. This method of hatching, with the head emerging first, is shared by nearly all birds. The only exceptions are a few waders and other ground-living birds, which either smash open their eggs in random pieces or kick their way out feet first.

7 INTO THE OUTSIDE WORLD

With a final push, the chick tumbles out of the shell that has protected it during the three and a half weeks of incubation. Within the next two hours, its feathers will dry and fluff up to provide an insulating jacket that will keep it warm. Once that has happened, the race is on to feed and grow. Pheasant chicks leave their nest almost immediately, and, amazing though it may seem, they are able to fly in only two weeks.

Growing up

GROUND-NESTING BIRDS hatch in a well-developed state (p. 56). However, the newly hatched young of many tree- and hole-nesting birds are little more than baglike feeding machines. They have well-developed digestive systems, but everything else about them - including their eyes - is unfinished. This does not last for long. Fueled by a staggering supply of food, nestlings like the blue tit's grow at a great rate. The young of many species increase their weight by ten times in as many days, and their development is so rapid that they quickly catch up with birds that hatch with all their feathers.

Wing

Leg

Mouth brightly colored to attract attention

Feather tufts

Joined eyelids

Feather tract   *Feather sheaths*

1 ONE DAY OLD
Twenty-four hours after hatching, blue tit nestlings have no feathers and their eyes are closed. During the day, both parents leave the nestlings to search for food. However, the young never remain on their own for long, because their parents return to the nest with food every few minutes. The parents may make up to 1,000 trips between them per day.

BIRD OF GOOD OMEN
Faithful to its mate and tireless as a parent, the stork is recognized internationally as a symbol of the birth of a new human baby.

2 THREE DAYS OLD
In a scene all too familiar to their weary parents, the growing nestlings beg for food. Their instinctive reaction is set off by their parents' arrival at the nest, or sometimes by the parents' calls. By the third day, small tufts of feathers have appeared, and the nestlings are about four times heavier than when they hatched.

3 FIVE DAYS OLD
By this time, dark gray feather tracts have appeared down the nestlings' backs and on their wings. These are the areas of skin that will produce feathers. On the wings, the tubelike sheaths that will eventually produce and protect the flight feathers have already started to develop.

ESCAPE FROM DANGER
Although most birds protect their nestlings by bluff or aggression when threatened, some parents can pick up their young and carry them away. Depending on the species, they may use either their beak, legs, or talons.

EMERGENCY AIRLIFT
The woodcock is said to hold a chick between its legs while flying, although this has never been proved.

PINCER MOVEMENT
The secretive water rail carries its chicks in its long beak.

CARRIED IN TALONS
Some birds of prey, like the buzzard, are thought to hold their nestlings in their talons.

Feather sheaths

Emerging feather tips

4 NINE DAYS OLD
As the feather sheaths grow longer, the tips of the flight feathers themselves start to emerge. The areas of bare skin between the feather tracts have started to disappear, covered up by the growing feathers. The nest is starting to get crowded, although by blue tit standards, five nestlings is a relatively small family.

5 THIRTEEN DAYS OLD
At nearly two weeks, the nestlings are fully feathered and their eyes are open. Within another five days they will leave the nest, but the young birds will follow their parents for some time, begging for food as they gradually learn how to look after themselves. Full independence often comes when the parents begin preparations for another clutch of eggs. Once the young birds find that their parents are ignoring their calls for food, they fend for themselves.

Attracting birds

I̲N WINTER, A ROOSTING BIRD like a robin can burn up a tenth of its body weight just in order to stay alive during the long hours of darkness. With each chilly daybreak, the hungry bird must find food soon or die, so there is no better way to attract birds into your backyard than by providing a regular supply of winter food. Seeds, nuts, fat, kitchen scraps, and water will not only help the birds but will also enable you to watch them at close quarters. Having kept your backyard birds alive during the winter, you can persuade many to stay for the summer by giving them somewhere to nest. As wild habitats disappear, nest boxes placed carefully beyond the reach of cats make valuable homes for a variety of birds.

Great and blue tits are attracted by nuts and fat at bird tables

CALL OF THE WILD
Birds have an instinctive distrust of humans, but St. Francis of Assisi (here portrayed in stained glass) is said to have had a special attraction for birds.

GABLED BOXES
A roof gives nestlings protection aginst rain, but it also reduces air circulation. Nest boxes should not be placed where they will be in direct sunlight.

Sloping lid to throw off rainwater

Hole 1.14 in (29 mm) across keeps out large birds

Perching post

SIMPLE HOLE-FRONTED BOXES
This straightforward design appeals to woodland birds such as tits and nuthatches. The small hole keeps out inquisitive sparrows.

Hinged lid for inspecting nest

OPEN-FRONT BOXES
Robins, flycatchers, wrens, and wagtails prefer nest boxes that give them a good view when incubating. These birds usually nest in thick vegetation, so the box needs to be well concealed. This will also help to protect the birds from cats.

Removable lid for inspecting nest

Two halves of a log hollowed out and nailed together to make the nesting chamber

LOG BOXES
A hollowed-out log makes an excellent home for small woodland birds. This box does not have a perching post, but the bark around the entrance hole is rough enough to give a bird a good toe-hold when landing or taking off.

FANCY BOXES
What appeals to humans doesn't necessarily appeal to birds. Bird boxes with unnecessary decorations may put birds off looking for a home. If you do choose a "house box" like this, first make sure that it is solidly built. Then check that it can be cleaned and that the roof really will keep rainwater out of the nesting chamber.

Feeding table may attract other birds, disturbing those nesting in the box

MEALWORMS
Insect-eating birds find these beetle grubs quite irresistible. Mealworms can be raised in containers filled with bran.

Great spotted woodpecker feeding on peanuts

Screw-fit lid for refilling

Peanuts

Perching post

Wire mesh keeping nuts in and large birds out

Fat and seed ball

Commercial "bird pudding"

LOOSE SEED
Mixtures of loose seed are an excellent food, although birds such as tits may fly away with the larger seeds and eat them out of sight.

SEED CAKES AND PUDDINGS
Of all the kinds of food that you can give backyard birds, oils and fats are the best sources of energy. All seeds have oils in them, but they can be pressed together with more oil or fat to make a real bird banquet. This way of feeding birds has another advantage. Because the food is in a solid lump, birds cannot fly away with it, giving you plenty of opportunity to watch them at their meal.

Seed cake

Coconut, a winter food for acrobatic blue tits

Hunger sometimes forces birds to overcome shyness in winter

NUT DISPENSER
Natural, *unsalted* peanuts are popular with tits and greenfinches. A hanging dispenser helps to keep larger birds at bay.

BREAD
Although not an ideal food for birds, bread makes a useful stop-gap. Brown bread makes a far better bird food than white.

Watching birds

IN NORTH AMERICA ALONE, including annual migrants, there are about 900 species of birds. An experienced bird watcher may recognize any one of these given no more than a distant silhouette or just a few seconds of song. This skill can seem baffling, but it is simply the result of careful observation - looking at the shape and color of birds and also watching the way they live.

Getting close to wild birds requires skill and patience

WARNING
When watching birds, always avoid disturbing them. Be especially careful when watching or photographing parent birds with their young.

KEEPING A NOTEBOOK
Field guides are essential for identifying birds, but keeping a notebook is the best way to train your eye to look for a bird's key features. Sketching plumage and flight patterns and noting behavior will all help to build up your knowledge.

SKETCHING EQUIPMENT
You don't have to be an artist to draw birds. A collection of colored pencils will enable you to sketch details instead of writing lengthy notes

Ruler for measuring feathers

Objective lens

Eyepiece lens

BINOCULARS
Serious bird watching is almost impossible without a good pair of binoculars, but good does not necessarily mean tremendously powerful. For bird watching, binoculars should be light and have good magnification together with a fairly wide field of view. Heavy binoculars are hard to carry and use, and if they magnify more than 10 times, the field of view is narrow and the image very wobbly - this can make locating moving birds very difficult. Binoculars are graded by the diameter of the objective lens and the magnification. One of the best combinations of size and magnification for bird watching is the 8 x 30

Plastic tweezers are less likely to damage fine bones than metal ones

Magnifying glass

Buzzard feather

STORING FEATHERS

Paper or plastic bags prevent feathers from becoming damaged.

Pigeon feathers

Shearwater feather

EQUIPMENT FOR EXAMINING PELLETS

Many of the animal remains inside bird pellets (p. 42) are very delicate and are easily damaged when a pellet is pulled apart. By using a magnifying glass and a pair of tweezers, small bones and teeth can be separated from fur and feathers without breakage.

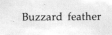
Camera mounting

TRIPOD

Cameras that use high-power lenses need a steady support to keep the image from wobbling. A lightweight tripod is essential. It can also be used with binoculars.

USING A "HIDE"

Birds are quick to detect movement but will ignore nonmoving objects, no matter how out of place they seem to human eyes. Even on flat, open ground birds will accept a "hide" as a natural feature and approach it without any fear.

CHOOSING LENSES

With a standard 50 mm lens, birds often appear small and indistinct. A telephoto lens produces a much larger image.

CAMERAS FOR BIRD PHOTOGRAPHY

A 35 mm SLR (single-lens reflex) camera is ideal for photographing birds because the image can be seen exactly through the viewfinder. Taking pictures of wild birds - especially in flight - *is* difficult. Practice approaching the subject, focusing quickly, and steadying the camera - before going farther afield.

200 mm tele-photo lens

Did you know?

FASCINATING FACTS

There are over 9,500 species of birds in the world, and they live nearly everywhere, from icebergs to deserts, making them the most widespread of all animals. About two-thirds of all the bird species are found in tropical rain forests.

Hoatzin

Hoatzin chicks have two claws on each wing. When the chicks climb out of the nest, they use their claws to cling onto mangrove trees. Once the birds have grown, they lose their claws, but they are never very good at flying.

Owls cannot swivel their huge eyes. Instead, they can turn their heads completely around to see straight behind them.

Swans have up to 25,000 feathers—the most feathers of any bird. Some hummingbirds, on the other hand, are so small that they have fewer than 1,000.

Brown kiwi

Kiwis are unique in having nostrils right at the end of their beaks so they can sniff for food, such as worms and insects, on the ground. Every now and then, they snort to clear their nostrils.

Instead of singing, a woodpecker drums its beak against a tree. Other woodpeckers know which bird it is by the sound of the drumming.

The most talkative bird in the world is the African gray parrot. One bird was such a good mimic that it could say 800 words.

The marsh warbler is a talented mimic. It can copy the songs of more than 80 different birds.

Secretary bird eating a snake

The secretary bird, which lives on African grasslands, often eats snakes. It kills them by stamping on them, and uses its wings as a shield to protect itself from being bitten.

The pelican's huge, pouchlike beak can hold up to 2.5 gallons (10 liters) of water at a time. The beak shrinks to squeeze out the water before the pelican swallows its catch.

The lammergeier, a vulture, carries bones high into the air, then drops them onto rocks. It then eats the smashed bones, taking them into its mouth like a circus sword swallower.

Instead of making a nest, the Mallee fowl builds a huge compost heap in which the female lays her eggs. The eggs then incubate in the heat given off by the rotting vegetation.

Social weaver birds live in a huge communal nest like a haystack spread across a treetop. The nest may be 100 years old, weigh a few tons, and have 400 birds living in it.

The condor's giant wings are used for gliding; it hardly has to flap its wings at all.

Condor

The Andean condor is the heaviest bird of prey, weighing up to 27 lb (12 kg). It spirals high in the sky on warm thermals rising from the mountains below.

The shimmering colors on the tail feathers of the male peacock are actually an impression caused by layers of pigment that reflect and split light.

Like many gorgeous male birds, the Count Raggi's bird of paradise is polygamous. No sooner has it mated with one female, than it starts displaying again to win the attention of another.

Count Raggi's bird of paradise

QUESTIONS AND ANSWERS

Q What is the most common wild bird in the world?

A The red-billed quelea is the world's most numerous wild bird. Over 1.5 billion of them live in Africa, which means that at the moment, there are about a quarter as many red-billed queleas as there are people in the world.

Peregrine

Q Which bird can fly the fastest?

A When a peregrine falcon swoops down on its prey in a steep dive, it averages speeds of over 110 mph (180 kph), making it the fastest-flying bird.

Q How long do birds live, and which bird lives the longest?

A About 75% of wild birds live for less than a year. Some of the largest birds live the longest. The large wandering albatross can live for up to 80 years.

Q Which birds are best at swimming?

A Gentoo penguins are the fastest swimmers, reaching speeds of 22 mph (36 kph). Emperor penguins can stay underwater for up to 18 minutes.

Emperor penguin

Q Which birds spend the most time in the air?

A The sooty tern is the most aerial bird. It takes off over the oceans and flies for at least 3 years without ever settling on water or land. Swifts also spend most of their lives in the air, only landing when they are going to nest. They even sleep on the wing, continuing to glide on air currents with their wings outstretched.

Q Which bird makes the longest journey when migrating?

A Arctic terns fly right across the world and back every year, so they make the longest annual migration of any bird. They fly 25,000 miles (40,000 km) from the Arctic to the Antarctic and then back again.

Q How do migrating birds find their way across the world?

A Migrating birds follow the same routes every year, but nobody knows exactly how. They may use the position of the Sun and stars to help them find their way, or they may follow prominent features in the landscape below them, such as coastlines and mountains. Some people think they might also use the Earth's magnetic fields for guidance.

Penguins use their small, stiff wings like flippers to propel them through the water.

Wingspan of up to 11.8 ft (3.63 m)

Wandering albatross

Q Why do some birds have huge wings?

A The wandering albatross has the greatest wingspan of any bird. It spends most of its life above the ocean, using its huge wings to soar in light winds. Being able to glide for a long time means it can cover great distances without having to use up too much energy.

Q How high in the sky can birds fly?

A Many geese and swans fly very high when migrating. Bar-headed geese fly across the Himalayas, the highest mountains in the world, when migrating from their summer breeding grounds to their winter feeding grounds in India. They fly nearly 5 miles (over 8,000 m) up in the sky—nearly as high as jet planes.

Record Breakers

BIGGEST BIRD
The ostrich is the largest, tallest, and heaviest bird of all. Male ostriches are up to 9 ft (2.7 m) tall and weigh up to 350 lb (160 kg).

SMALLEST BIRD
The bee hummingbird of Cuba is the smallest bird in the world. At just over 2 in (5.7 cm) long, it is not much bigger than a bumblebee.

FASTEST LEVEL FLIGHT
The spine-tailed swift and the red-breasted merganser (a duck) have been credited with flying at 100 mph (161 kph) in level flight.

SLOWEST BIRD
The American woodcock flies at 5 mph (8 kph), slower than any other bird.

BIGGEST TREE NEST
The bald eagle builds the largest tree nest, measuring 9½ ft (2.9 m) across.

SMALLEST NEST
The vervain hummingbird builds the smallest nest. It only measures a half inch (1.5 cm) across.

Snowy Owl

Identifying birds

To make identification easier, birds are divided into groups, based on features that they have in common, such as their physical features and behavior. The biggest groups are called orders. They are divided into smaller groups, called families. Here are some major bird orders and their key characteristics.

BIRD ORDERS

FLIGHTLESS BIRDS

Several orders of birds contain species that run, but cannot fly. On land, they include ostriches, rheas, and cassowaries—large, long-legged birds that escape their enemies by running away. Flightless land birds also include much smaller kinds, such as the kiwi, which comes out to feed at night. At sea, the most common flightless birds are penguins. Penguins are only found in the southern hemisphere.

Strong legs and two-toed feet enable the ostrich to run fast

Ostrich

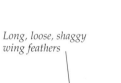

Long, loose, shaggy wing feathers

Strong legs and short, thick toes

Rhea

LARGE WADING BIRDS

Many birds wade into water to find their food. The largest of them include herons, spoonbills, egrets, and flamingos. These birds all have long legs and feet with slender toes, and extra-long necks for reaching down into the water. Most of these birds eat fish and crustaceans, and the shapes of their beaks vary, depending on how they catch their food.

Round-ended, spoon-shaped bill, which is swept sideways through the water

Roseate spoonbill

Stiltlike legs, typical of the larger waders

Juvenile greater flamingo

Dagger-shaped bill characteristic of many fish-eating birds

Black-crowned night heron

WATERFOWL

Swans, geese, and ducks are waterfowl and live near ponds, lakes, and rivers. They have webbed feet, three forward-pointing toes and ducklike beaks. Swans are the largest of this group. Geese are smaller, often fly in a "V" formation and make honking calls. Ducks have short necks. Their feet are set far back on their bodies, causing them to waddle when they walk.

Long, flexible neck and snowy white plumage

Mute swan

Stocky build and upright stance typical of geese.

Chinese goose

Bold markings, like a uniform, distinguish one type of duck from another

Common shelduck

66

BIRD ORDERS

BIRDS OF PREY

Often called raptors, birds of prey are meat-eating hunters with strong, hooked beaks, excellent eyesight and long legs armed with fierce talons. They attack prey feet-first, catching them with their talons, then tearing them apart using their beaks. There are two different families of birds of prey. One includes kites, hawks, eagles, and buzzards, while the other includes falcons, such as the kestrel.

Wings designed for hovering while scouring the ground for prey

Kestrel

Powerful, hooked beak

Bald eagle

GAME BIRDS

Pheasants, grouse, partridges and quails are all game birds. Starling-to-chicken sized, they have stout bodies and small heads with chickenlike beaks. They spend most of their time on the ground, often feeding on seeds, but they take to the air when in danger, jumping straight up, then flying off with a distinctive whirring style.

Long, trailing tail feathers

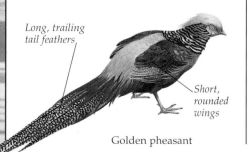

Short, rounded wings

Golden pheasant

SHOREBIRDS AND WADERS

This large order of birds includes seagulls, terns, small wading birds, puffins, and guillemots. Most of them have long, spindly legs, compact bodies, and thin, probing beaks. They live on coasts, marshland, and mud flats. Some of them feed at the edge of the water, while others catch their food from the sea.

Long, narrow wings for fast flight

Arctic tern

PARROTS

The parrot order includes parrots, lorikeets, cockatoos, and macaws. They are colorful, noisy birds that live in tropical rain forests or on open plains. Parrots have strong, hooked beaks and four toes, two at the front and two at the back. Most of them feed on nuts, berries, leaves, and flowers. They usually live in flocks and screech noisily to each other.

Strong, hooked beak can crack open nuts

Macaw

Brightly colored plumage

Lovebird

OWLS

Owls are predators, usually nocturnal, with large, round heads, flat faces, and hooked beaks. Their large round eyes give them excellent night vision. They have fringed wing feathers for silent flight and strong, sharp talons for catching prey.

Southern boobook owl

KINGFISHERS AND HOOPOES

This order also includes hornbills, kookaburras, rollers and bee-eaters. Most of the birds in this group are carnivorous land-dwellers. They have brightly colored, distinctive plumage and large beaks. Many of them feed on insects and other small creatures. Kingfishers plunge into freshwater to catch fish.

Green wood-hoopoe

PERCHING BIRDS

This bird order contains over half of all the bird species, including swallows, thrushes, warblers, tits, and crows. Perching birds have four toes on each foot, three facing forward and one at the back, to give them a firm grip on branches.

Blue tit

Golden oriole

Find out more

WHEREVER YOU LIVE, there are always birds to watch. You can learn a lot about them simply by observing those in the area around your home, but to see different varieties, you will need to visit different habitats. Going for a walk in the country or by the sea can introduce you to many interesting new species. You could visit bird reserves, sanctuaries, and zoos to come into contact with more rare and unusual birds.

BIRD SANCTUARIES
Visiting bird sanctuaries, such as this hawk conservancy in Hampshire, England, gives you the opportunity to see rare and nocturnal birds, such as hawks and owls, at close hand. These organizations often put on flying demonstrations as well.

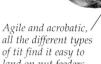

Nuts and seeds attract blue tits to a garden.

Agile and acrobatic, all the different types of tit find it easy to land on nut feeders.

It is easy to identify a blue tit by the bright blue on the top of its head and wings.

Blue tits

Swans at a wildfowl and wetlands center

WETLANDS
Lakes, rivers, swamps, and marshes are home to a wide variety of birds, from swans and ducks to herons and storks. Here, food is plentiful and there are safe nesting places in reeds and on the banks. Many birds rest in wetland areas when migrating.

PARKS AND GARDENS
The parks and gardens in towns and cities are good places to look for different birds. With their trees, flowerbeds, and ponds, they provide a wealth of different habitats. Putting out food for the birds can attract many different species to your garden, balcony, or window ledge, especially in winter, when food is scarce in the country.

ZOOS
One of the best places to see exotic and tropical birds at close hand is in aviaries at zoos. Many large zoos have different avaries for birds from different habitats. Lorikeet Landing at the San Diego Zoo is a small aviary where flocks of lorikeets fly among visitors. Visitors can buy small cups of nectar so that the birds feed straight from their hands.

Lorikeets at San Diego Zoo, California

Places to visit

YELLOWSTONE NATIONAL PARK, WYOMING
A wide range of birds can be found at the different elevations within the park.

FLORIDA EVERGLADES, FLORIDA
The Greater Flamingo and coastal birds, including, Shortailed Hawks, Great Blue Herons, and Bald Eagles live here.

JAMAICA BAY WILDLIFE REFUGE, NEW YORK
More than 330 species have been seen in this Queens park, a popular stop along many migration routes.

POINT REYES NATIONAL SEASHORE, SAN FRANCISCO, CALIFORNIA
Home to a wide range of species, from hawks and other birds of prey to seabirds such as Oystercatchers.

Crimson rosella

TROPICAL FORESTS

When on vacation, it is well worth visiting the national parks in different places to see native species of birds and plants you might not see at home. The magnificent rain forests and eucalyptus forests of Lamington National Park in Queensland, Australia are home to many species of colorful tropical birds. There you can see cockatoos, lorikeets, lyrebirds, and the crimson rosella, all of which feed on the fruit, flowers, and insects that are abundant year round.

FOREST AND WOODLAND

With plenty of buds, berries, seeds, and insects to eat and safe places to nest, forests and woodlands provide a rich habitat for birds. Generally, more birds live in deciduous woodlands than in dark conifer forests. This is because there is a greater variety of trees there and it is often warmer and wetter. Many birds can live together in woodlands because they feed at different levels in the trees, sharing the available food. Many of them nest in tree holes.

Golden-fronted woodpecker

Gannet colony

SEASHORE AND CLIFFS

The coast is a good place to look out for gulls and other seabirds, especially during the breeding season in spring. Many birds flock to tall cliffs and rocky offshore islands to nest where their eggs and chicks will be safe from predators. Away from the cliffs, dunes and beaches also provide nesting places for birds. Look out for waders feeding on worms and shellfish in the shallow waters of estuaries, particularly in winter.

USEFUL WEB SITES

● The National Audubon Society works to protect birds and their natural habitats:
www.audubon.org

● Wild Bird Centers of America provides extensive information about feeding birds in your own backyard:
www.birdfeeding.org

● BirdSource features information about identifying birds. Visitors can participate in online bird counting projects:
www.birdsource.org

Identifying birds by their flight silhouette

The size and shape of a bird's wings suits its lifestyle. Look out for these flight silhouettes to help you identify the birds you see.

NARROW, TAPERING WINGS
Birds that fly fast, such as martins, swallows, and swifts, have slender, tapering wings and forked tails that help them to maneuver quickly.

LONG, ELEGANT WINGS
Terns and other seabirds that spend a lot of time in the air have long, narrow, pointed wings. This shape enables them to glide on currents of air.

BACKWARD-POINTING WINGS
Falcons and other small birds of prey have narrow tails and narrow, pointed wings that are swept backward for high-speed flying.

MASSIVE WINGSPAN
Long-distance gliders, such as albatrosses and shearwaters, have very long, narrow, pointed wings. They glide across the open sea on warm currents of rising air.

FEATHERED FINGERS
Eagles, buzzards, and vultures have large, wide wings with splayed "fingers" at the tips for gliding at slow speeds and for soaring.

SHORT, ROUNDED WINGS
Sparrowhawks, jays, and many woodland birds have short, wide, rounded wings so they can fly in and out of trees easily. They use their tails like brakes when landing.

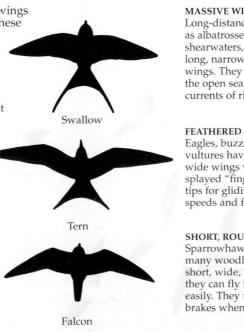

Swallow

Tern

Falcon

Albatross

Eagle

Sparrowhawk

Glossary

AIRFOIL The wing cross section that enables a bird to fly. The wing is flat underneath, but the upper surface is slightly curved from front to back. The airflow over and beneath the wing produces lift.

ALULA A tuft of feathers on the leading edge of a bird's wing that it raises to prevent the bird from stalling as it slows down

BAR A natural colored mark or stripe across a feather or group of feathers

BARBS Tiny side branches off a feather shaft that make up a bird's feather

BINOCULAR VISION The area of sight in which the fields of vision of both eyes overlap. Binocular vision enables birds to judge distances accurately.

BODY FEATHERS Sometimes also called contour feathers, these are the small, overlapping feathers on a bird's head and body that give it a streamlined shape.

BREED To lay eggs and raise chicks

BREEDING SEASON The time of year when birds mate, build nests, lay eggs, and raise their chicks

BROOD PATCH A bare area of skin on the underside of a bird's body that it lays against its eggs to keep them warm while they are incubating

CAMOUFLAGE The color and patterning of a bird's feathers that match its particular surroundings, making it hard to see

CASQUE A hard, hornlike projection either on top of a bird's head (cassowary) or on its beak (hornbill)

CLUTCH The total number of eggs that is incubated by a parent bird or a pair of birds at any one time

A gannet colony

Body feather

COLONY A large group of birds that lives together in one place to breed or roost, or the place in which they live

COURTSHIP The behavior of birds when finding partners before mating. It may take the form of special movements, dancing, or songs.

COVERTS Groups of small feathers that cover the base of the main flight feathers

CREPUSCULAR Active at twilight or just before dawn, when the light is dim

CROP A bag-like extension of a bird's gut used to store food. It is often used to carry food back to the nest.

CROWN The top of a bird's head

DABBLING The way a duck feeds, by opening and shutting its beak while skimming it across the surface of the water

DISPLAY A conspicuous pattern of movements used to communicate with other birds of the same species, especially during courtship or when threatened

DISTRIBUTION All the areas in which a bird is seen regularly

DIURNAL Active during the daytime, when it is light

DOWN FEATHERS Very soft, fine feathers that trap air close to a bird's body and help to keep it warm

EGG TOOTH A small structure on the tip of a chick's upper bill, which it uses to crack open the eggshell when hatching. The egg tooth drops off soon after hatching.

EXTINCTION The process by which a species of living things, such as the dodo, dies out completely and no longer exists

FIELD GUIDE A pocket-sized book that helps the reader to identify different birds

FLEDGE To grow a full set of feathers

FLEDGLING A young bird that has grown its first set of feathers and has left the nest. It may not be able to fly right away.

FLIGHT FEATHERS The long feathers that make up a bird's wings and are used to fly. They can be grouped into primary feathers (on the outer wing) and secondary feathers (on the inner wing).

FLOCK A group of birds of the same species flying or feeding together

FORAGE To search an area for food of some kind

Blue tit nestlings

GIZZARD The muscular chamber in a bird's stomach where the plant material that it has eaten is ground into a pulp

HABITAT The type of environment where a bird is normally found, such as wetland, forest, or grassland

HATCHING The process by which a baby bird breaks out of its egg by chipping its way through the shell with the tiny egg tooth on its beak

Chick hatching

Hide at a bird reserve

Seabird in flight

NECTAR The sweet liquid produced by a flower to attract birds and insects to feed from the flower and so pollinate it at the same time

NESTLING A baby bird that is still in the nest and cannot fly

NOCTURNAL Active by night

ORNITHOLOGIST A person who studies birds. Professional ornithologists work in bird observatories, museums, and universities or for conservation organizations.

PELLET A hard lump of indigestible bits of food, such as fur and bones, that birds such as owls cough up

PLUMAGE A bird's feathers   Pellets

POWDER DOWN Special feathers on some birds, such as egrets and herons, that disintegrate to form a powder, which the bird uses to clean its plumage and keep it in good condition

PRECOCIAL Down-covered baby birds that have their eyes open and leave the nest soon after hatching

PREDATOR A bird or animal that kills other birds or animals for food

PREENING The way in which birds keep their feathers in good condition, drawing them through their beaks to clean and smooth them

PREY A bird or animal that is hunted and killed by another animal

PRIMARY FEATHERS The long flight feathers on the outer half of a bird's wings, which it uses for steering and turning

QUILL The long, hollow central shaft of a bird's feather

REGURGITATE To bring food that has been swallowed back up into the mouth again. Many parent birds feed their chicks on regurgitated food.

ROOST To settle down to rest, normally overnight; also, a place where birds rest

RUMP The lower part of a bird's back, above the tail and beneath its closed wings

RUMP FEATHERS The soft, downy feathers above the base of a bird's tail

SCAVENGER A bird such as a vulture that searches for dead animals to eat

SCRAPE A nest hollow on the ground where a bird lays its eggs

SEABIRD Birds that spend most of their time over the open sea and only come ashore to breed

SECONDARY One of the inner wing feathers

SPECIES A group of similar birds that can breed together and have chicks

SPECULUM A white or brightly colored patch that some ducks have on each wing

STOOP To swoop down (bird of prey)

TALONS The sharp, curved claws of a bird of prey

TENDON A band of tough tissue connecting a muscle to a bone

A goose preening its feathers

TERRITORY An area occupied by a bird that it may defend against other birds of the same species

TERTIALS A bird's innermost flight feathers, which shape the wing into the body to ensure a smooth flight

THERMAL A rising column of warm air, often at the edge of a cliff or hillside, on which soaring birds glide to take themselves higher into the sky

VERTEBRATE Any animal that has a backbone. Birds are vertebrates.

WETLANDS Swamps, marshes, and other wet areas of land

WILDFOWL A wide range of web-footed birds found in, on, or near water, such as ducks, geese, and swans

HIDE A structure or small building where people can hide to watch birds without being seen by the birds or disturbing them

INCUBATION Providing constant warmth for eggs so that chicks can develop inside them. Most birds incubate their eggs by sitting on them to keep them warm.

INVERTEBRATE A type of small animal that has no backbone, such as a worm, an insect, a spider, or a crab

IRIDESCENT The glittering sheen on some feathers and other objects that appears to change color depending on the direction that the light is coming from

JUVENILE A young bird that is not yet old enough to breed. Its plumage often differs in color and pattern from that of an adult.

JUVENILE PLUMAGE A bird's first set of feathers, with which it leaves the nest

KEEL A large, plate-like extension of a flying bird's breastbone, which anchors its powerful wing muscles in place

KERATIN A type of protein from which feathers, hair, nails, and hooves are made

LEK A communal display site where male birds of some species gather to display to females during the breeding season

MANDIBLE One of the two parts of a bird's beak. The upper mandible is the top part of the beak, and the lower mandible is the bottom part.

MIGRANT A bird that travels from its feeding grounds to its breeding grounds once a year and then back again

MIGRATE To travel from one place to another in search of a plentiful food supply or good breeding grounds

MONOCULAR VISION The area seen by one eye only, rather than by both eyes working together. In monocular vision, the fields of vision of both eyes do not overlap.

MOLTING Shedding worn-out feathers and growing new ones in their place

Index

Acknowledgments

The publisher would like to thank:
Phyilip Amies; the staff of the Natural History Department, City of Bristol Museum; the staff of the British Museum Natural History) at Tring; Martin Brown of the Wildfowl Trust, Slimbridge; and Rosemary Crawford for their advice and invaluable help in providing specimens; Steve Parker and Anne-Marie Bulat for their work on the initial stages of the book; Fred Ford and Mike Pilley of Radius Graphics, and Ray Owen and Nick Madren for artwork; Tim Hammond for editoral assistance.

Publisher's note:
No bird has been injured or in any way harmed during the preparation of this book.

For this edition, the publisher would also like to thank: the author for assisting with revisions; Claire Bowers, David Ekholm–JAlbum, Sunita Gahir,

Joanne Little, Nigel Ritchie, Susan St. Louis, Carey Scott, and Bulent Yusuf for the clip art; David Ball, Neville Graham, Rose Horridge, Joanne Little, and Sue Nicholson for the wall chart.

The publisher would like to thank the following for their kind permission to reproduce their images:

Picture credits: t=top, b=bottom, c=center, l=left, r=right.

Ardea London: Tony & Liz Bomfod 14mr.
Bridgeman Art Library: 13tr; 28tr; 52t; 61b.
Bruce Coleman Ltd: 64cl; Johnny Johnson 65bl; Gordon Langsbury 13b; 14b; Allan G. Potts 69tr; Robert Wilmshurst 15b.
Mary Evans Picture Library: 6bl; br; 9tr; mr; 10t, mr, b; 20bl; 24t; 26t; 30mr; 32m; 36t, mr; 38t; 41t; 54tl, tr, bl; 56t; 58b.
Gables: 66-67bkg; 70-71bkg.

Sonia Halliday: 60tr.
Robert Harding: Brian Hawkes 47t.
Frank Lane Picture Agency: 12bl; 14m, 16t; 29t, ml; 33b, 35tr, 37mr, bl, tl, 46m, 47m; 60tl, m, 63; R. Austing 32 br; C. Carvalho17t; J.K. Fawcett 12mr; T. & P. Gardner 21bl; John Hawkins 13tl; 19tl; 35m; Peggy Heard 61m; R. Jones 17m; Derek A. Robinson 8m, 47b; H. Schrempp 32bl; Roger Tidman 36tr; B.S. Turner 42t; R. Van Tidman 37br; John Watkins/ Tidman 33ml; Robert Wilmshurst/ Tidman 12 br; 46t; 49t; W. Wisniewski/ Tidman 37ml; J. Zimmermann/ Tidman 31tr; 36b.
Natural History Museum: 70cl, cr, bl, 71ca, bl.
NHPA: Bruce Beehler 64br; G.I. Bernard 21ml, mr; Manfred Danegger 13m; Hellio & Van Ingen 40b; Michael Leach 34m; Crimson Rosella 69tl; Jonathan and Angela Scott 64c; Philip Wayre 19br; Alan Williams 68cr.
Mansell Collection: 6t, 10ml; 34t; 54m.

Oxford Scientific Films: Richard Herrmann 68bc; Ronald Toms 68tl.
Pickthall Library: 15t.
Planet Earth Pictures: A.P. Barnes 15m.
Press-Tige Pictures: 12mr.
Science Photo Library: Sinclair Stammers 6m.
South of England Rare Breed Centre: 66crb.
Survival Anglia: Jen & Des Bartlett 54br; Jeff Foott 31mr.
Alan Williams: 71tl.
Jerry Young: 66tl.

Jacket credits: Front: B: John Foxx/Alamy; tc: © Natural History Museum, London, England

Wall chart: DK Images: Natural History Museum, London ca, crb, tr.

All other images © Dorling Kindersley. For further information see:
www.dkimages.com